EXTRAORDINARY LIVES

Celebrating
50 years of the
Irish Wheelchair
Association

EXTRAORDINARY LIVES

Celebrating
50 years of the
Irish Wheelchair
Association

Written and edited by Joanna Marsden

Contemporary photography by Paul Sherwood

IWA archive research by Mairéad Farquharson & Anita Matthews

Extraordinary Lives
CONTENTS

Foreword
by President Mary McAleese

The Irish Wheelchair Association was born out of the vision and dedication of a small number of inspiring people. Today it boasts a membership of 20,000 and is evidence of what can be achieved when individuals combine to improve their lives and to remove the unnecessary obstacles which stand in the way of achieving their fullest potential.

If ever a group of people could tell the story of moving from social exclusion to social, civic and political inclusion, it is wheelchair users. How long and hard they had to lobby to shift the many obstacles – physical, legal and attitudinal – which kept them from living life on their own terms. When this organisation started fifty years ago, the road ahead was something of an isolated and overlooked by-road that just ran into more by-roads and even cul-de-sacs. The structural, attitudinal, legal and systemic changes we have witnessed over these past fifty years have not brought about a world of perfection for wheelchair users, but they have certainly changed the landscape of experience and opportunity for the better. They have brought issues like access, care, opportunity and rights into the mainstream of civic discourse nationally, at European level and internationally.

An Association is only as strong as the determination of its members and this Association is very strong indeed. The many inspiring voices who have contributed their own personal story to these pages are moving testimony to the long brave journey that had to be travelled to reach the Ireland of today, where people with disabilities live and work alongside able bodied neighbours and colleagues, making huge contributions to the community and to the worlds of politics, religion, business, arts, finance, public service, entrepreneurship, sport, and so many more areas of society.

As the Irish Wheelchair Association celebrates this golden jubilee, its members can look back on a story of remarkable achievement and success. I hope it fuels the energy, courage and commitment that will be needed to keep up the momentum of transformation over the next fifty years. Thank you for all you have done to enhance the lives of individuals, to educate our society and to help our country honour its ambition to be a place that cherishes all its children equally.

Mary McAleese

MARY McALEESE
PRESIDENT OF IRELAND

Introduction
by Kathleen Mc Loughlin

Welcome to *Extraordinary Lives*, a book which has been written to commemorate the 50th anniversary of the founding of the Irish Wheelchair Association. This book is much more than just a history of an organisation dedicated to improving life for people with disabilities, it is a book which in many ways reflects the social history of the nation. I like to think of this book as a 'story' book, filled with stories about ordinary people doing extraordinary things, living extraordinary lives and achieving at an extraordinary level.

Through their stories, we learn about the foundation of the Association and the vision, ambition and determination of the founding members who set about changing attitudes, beliefs and expectations for people with disabilities. We learn also of the experiences of people who grew up in an Ireland where services for people with disabilities were either limited, unsuitable or simply non-existent. We learn how, through the support of individual volunteers and communities across Ireland, the Association began to build alliances, develop services and influence the State to recognise the legitimate aspirations of people with disabilities.

The individuals who have participated in this project have given of their time freely and generously. They have bravely allowed us to use their stories to illustrate the reality of living with a disability in Ireland through the past five decades, and also to celebrate what can be achieved by individuals and communities working together with a shared vision. While each person is placed in a particular decade, we have taken some licence with this structure, allowing people to tell stories that span beyond a single decade. It is their life and their story, interwoven with the history of our Association, and we have deliberately edited very little from their interviews so that you, the reader, can hear the true voice of our contributors.

I hope you will enjoy reading about our unique organisation, its people and its history, and that you will celebrate with us all the positive changes for individuals and for society that have been made possible through the existence of the Irish Wheelchair Association.

KATHLEEN MC LOUGHLIN,
CHIEF EXECUTIVE OFFICER, IRISH WHEELCHAIR ASSOCIATION

OPPOSITE The Pillar Room at the Mater Hospital. It was in this room, on November 10th, 1960, that a group of wheelchair users met and, after much discussion and a vote on the options, decided to establish the Irish Wheelchair Association

A sincere thank you
From Gerry McMahon and Eileen O'Mahony

The Irish Wheelchair Association has grown and developed in a way that could not have been predicted by the founding members when they first met in November 1960. Over the course of IWA's history, the lives of countless Irish people have been improved through the work of the Association. In 2009 alone, 2.2 million hours of service were delivered to members of the Association. This figure does not include the many more thousands of hours that were delivered on a voluntary basis. The Association would like to acknowledge here the enormous support that it has enjoyed over the decades from Health Boards, HSE, FÁS, Government departments and generous benefactors who have donated funds and other resources towards our work.

We would also like to acknowledge the many other voluntary and community organisations that have worked with us and continue to work with us on a daily basis to support our members. They too can tell a similar tale of the challenges that have been faced over the years.

A very special thank you goes to the general public in communities right across Ireland who have never failed to support us in our efforts. For the time you have given and for the smallest donation to the largest bequest, we are truly indebted to all of you for allowing us to continue our work.

Above all, we would like to thank the individual staff, volunteers and members, who have given generously of their time and energy over the years. From the beginning, these individuals have shared a conviction that people with disabilities are entitled to more from life, and it is no exaggeration to say that they are the foundation upon which the Association is built. While it is impossible to name and acknowledge every individual in this book, we would like to take this opportunity to express our gratitude for the role each and every one of you played.

We hope that the next fifty years will see the Association continue to drive change, support members, advocate for improvements in services and create opportunities for people with disabilities. Our vital work must continue if we are to ensure that Irish people with disabilities are not excluded or on the margins of our society. Rather, we must ensure that every citizen can live an independent life, as an equal and participative member in every aspect of Irish society.

GERRY MCMAHON, CHAIRMAN, & EILEEN O'MAHONY, PRESIDENT

Acknowledgements

IWA would like to express its gratitude to the following people

for their generosity in contributing information or photographs for

this book. We would particularly like to thank Oliver Murphy and the families

of our founder members, including Bernie Grant, Brendan Close, Rosemary

Kerrigan, Joan Murphy, Terry Allen, John and Agnes Hayes, Willie and

Mary Hayes, Philip Hayes, Betty Rogers, Sheila O'Reilly, Anna Moore,

Agnes Brennan, the late Margaret Patton, Patrick Domican, Christy

Domican, Michael Clarke and Vanessa Carr. We would also

like to thank Peter Stokes, Phelim O'Reilly, Fr Paul Freeney,

Greg Harkin and All Hallows College.

This book is dedicated to all our members.

OPPOSITE IWA member John Twomey highlights the inaccessibility of a local cinema in 1979. In the 1970s, IWA began to lobby for improved accessibility to entertainment venues such as cinemas, theatres and museums

Members of the 1960 paralympic team arrive at Dublin Airport

SIMPLE BEGINNINGS

The story behind the foundation of the Irish Wheelchair Association

In 1960, life for people with disabilities in Ireland was very different from today. The majority of people with disabilities lived behind closed doors, in family homes, institutions or hospitals, and had little visible presence in society. Attitudes towards disability, however, were beginning to change. Medical advances such as antibiotics were resulting in increased longevity, particularly for those with spinal injuries, and Stoke Mandeville Hospital in the UK, led by Sir Ludwig Guttmann, was pioneering the concept of 'rehabilitation'. People had begun to talk about 'living with a disability', and in 1958, Ireland had started transforming its former tuberculosis hospital in Dun Laoghaire into a National Rehabilitation Hospital (NRH).

Fr Leo Close, who is recognised as the principal energy behind the establishment of the Irish Wheelchair Association, was a young seminarian in 1956, when he was paralysed in an accident while touring shrines in France. After being transferred to Stoke Mandeville for six months of intensive rehabilitation, he returned to Ireland with a determination to get on with life, resuming his studies and becoming the first wheelchair user to be ordained a priest in the Catholic Church in 1959.

Soon after his ordination, Fr Leo met wheelchair user Jack Kerrigan, who had been struggling with a spinal injury since 1949. Fr Leo encouraged Jack to go to Stoke Mandeville for rehabilitative care, where he became friends with Oliver Murphy, a young man from Drogheda who had acquired a spinal injury as a result of a work-related accident. Jack and Oliver also got to know a team of Irish nurses from the NRH, who had gone to Stoke Mandeville to train in rehabilitation nursing. These connections would help lay the foundation for the Irish Wheelchair Association and contribute to the spirit of friendship and collaboration that developed between NRH staff and IWA members in the early 1960s.

In September 1960, Fr Leo captained the Irish team, which included Jack and Oliver, as well as Jimmy Levins and Joan Horan, to the first Paralympic Games in Rome. "We spoke to an awful lot of people at the Games, particularly the Dutch and the Americans," remembers Oliver, "about how things were going in their countries. We formed the opinion – Fr Leo more than anyone else – that this was the time at home in Ireland when something should be started specifically to help people in wheelchairs." The Irish team returned inspired and uplifted by their experience and determined to act.

After a series of discussions between Fr Leo, Jack and Oliver in Drogheda, a meeting was organised for the evening of November 10th, 1960, in the Pillar Room at the Mater Hospital. This meeting, which would lead to the foundation of the Irish Wheelchair Association, was attended by Fr Leo, Jack, Oliver, Kay Hayes, Joe Domican, Joe Craven, Jimmy Levins, Fr Paddy Lewis, Joan Horan and Joe Davis. Fr Paddy Lewis later described Fr Leo, Jack and Oliver as "the trinity that began it all", but an important contribution was made by all the wheelchair users who debated the issues that evening, voting to found the Association and each subscribing ten shillings. In the years that followed, several of these founder members went on to play important roles in the development of IWA, and even those who played smaller roles continued to practise the philosophy behind the Association – one of independence, practicality and positivity – in their approach to life.

The Pillar Room Meeting

Founder member Jack Kerrigan, in an article dated September 3rd, 1981, remembered the meeting on November 10th, 1960, in the Pillar Room of the Mater Hospital, which resulted in the establishment of the Irish Wheelchair Association.

At 8pm on the evening of November 10th, 1960, ten people gathered around a table in the Pillar Room of the Mater Hospital in Dublin. They were there at the invitation of Fr Leo Close, to discuss the usefulness of existing organisations for the disabled and the need for one aimed specifically at helping wheelchair-bound people.

Two things, at least, all these people had in common. The first, they were all confined to wheelchairs; the second, they had all been helped by some other person in a wheelchair. Fr Leo opened the meeting by welcoming all and introducing them: Mrs Joan Horan, Mr Joe Davis, Mr Paddy Lewis, all patients in the hospital; Miss Kay Hayes, Clonard, Co Meath; Mr Joe Domican, Kill, Co Kildare; Mr Joe Craven, Mr Jimmy Levins, Mr Oliver Murphy and Mr Jack Kerrigan, all of Drogheda, Co Louth.

A little after 9pm, when all present had spoken, Fr Leo called for formal proposals. Jack Kerrigan proposed, and Oliver Murphy seconded: "That an organisation be formed to help people who were confined to wheelchairs." Joan Horan put forward a counter proposal: "That the group approach RTB [Rehabilitation of the Tuberculosis Group] with a request for their help." This proposal had no seconder. The first proposal was then put to the vote, resulting in eight votes in favour, one vote against, and one abstention. Paddy Lewis explained his position as being in favour, but as a student member of a religious order – needing his superiors' permission before joining any organisation, and his vote not being crucial – he abstained. Fr Leo declared the proposal carried and adjourned the meeting for a very welcome cup of tea. This was provided by the ever hospitable nuns.

After tea the meeting, now of eight people, resumed. Election of officers made Fr Leo, Chairman; Jack Kerrigan, Secretary; Oliver Murphy, Treasurer. Naming took very little time. Though most of the group were spinal injuries, this was regarded as too narrow a concept. The broader 'wheelchair' term covered the area in which we had some competence and most of those, including ourselves, who needed help.

Objectives were summarised as any possible activity that would benefit a wheelchair person. Structure was seen as a membership open to all those in wheelchairs deriving benefit. In view of travel difficulties, general meetings were restricted to quarterly. The officers were charged with meeting as often as possible, co-opting any interested persons who could be of service and getting on with recruitment, structure building and fundraising.

To start our fund, a subscription of ten shillings each was put in the 'kitty' in the centre of the table, and so ended the first meeting of the Irish Wheelchair Association.

The Pillar Room in the Mater Hospital

Before ending this article, I must explain that as first secretary, I recorded the above on the back of an envelope, transferring and filling it out the next day in a little red 'memo' note book. A few meetings later, a proper minute book was donated and the original thrown in a drawer in my bedroom. In the following year, I remember reading it once or twice and thinking it might be of interest some time in the future, so I put it somewhere 'safe'. Twenty years and three flittings later, I have no idea what became of it.

However, six of the original founders are still alive and well [including Fr Paddy Lewis], and I hope will comment on the accuracy of my recollection. One last fact not generally known is that there were quite a lot of other people in the Pillar Room that night, as well as the founder members.

I didn't record the names of the friends and relations who had helped with transport, but looking back I believe that Fr Leo's sister, Bernadette, Oliver Murphy's brother, Tony, Joe Craven's brother in law, Pat Lambe, Jimmy Levins' wife, Josie, Kay Hayes' sister, and Joe Domican's father and brother were all present though not seated at the table. It would be interesting to hear if any of them has a clear picture of the event.

Sincerely
Jack Kerrigan,
Dromahair, Co Leitrim
September 3rd, 1981

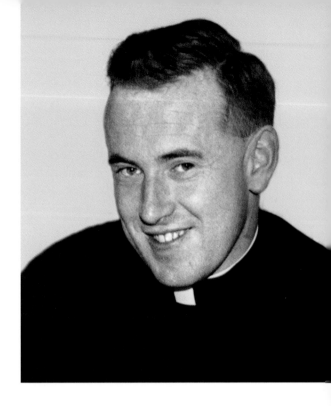

Fr Leo Close

A dynamic and ambitious man who greatly influenced the lives of others

1934 - 1977

Fr Leo Close is widely acknowledged as the driving force behind the foundation of IWA. In his relatively short life, he challenged the attitudes of the public, the universities and the Church, becoming the first wheelchair user in the world to be ordained as a Catholic priest. He exerted a remarkable personal influence on the other founder members of the Irish Wheelchair Association, instilling in them a belief that wheelchair users should expect more from life. In the words of Oliver Murphy, "If he didn't exist, I don't think IWA would be here."

Leo Close was born in Dublin in 1934, and educated at the Christian Brothers in Marino, at Belvedere College and at Mount St Joseph's Cistercian College in Roscrea. He was a bright student, who loved rugby and running, and performed in school productions of Gilbert and Sullivan. His father, also named Leo, was Chief Inspector of Schools and his mother, Kitty, was chairperson of the local Ladies Committee. He had an older brother, Brendan, and younger sister, Bernie. "He was known as León in the family because our father was Leo too," says Brendan.

In 1952, Leo joined the All Hallows Seminary, close to his home in Drumcondra. Run by the Vincentian Order, All Hallows prepared men to serve as priests in English-speaking countries around the world. Greg Harkin, the archivist at All Hallows, describes the order as "a privileged and well-educated group, who had great opportunity to travel and a tradition of independent thinking". Each student was sponsored by the diocese to which they would be assigned on ordination, and Leo's sponsor was the Bishop of Dunedin in South Island, New Zealand.

In the summer of 1956, Leo and five other clerical students went on a tour around France, visiting shrines such as Lisieux, Valence and Paray-le-Monial. Leo and his friend, Harry Costello, were sharing the driving, and one night they stopped on the outskirts of a small town called Moulin, in the Auvergne region. "It was about 10.30pm and they were planning on parking the car and finding a hostel in which to stay," says Bernie. "León got out of the car to have a look around and walked off into the darkness. Without realising, he walked onto the remains of an old bridge which had been bombed in the Second World War, and he fell into the sixty foot ravine below. His fall was broken by a tree, saving his life but leaving him paralysed from the waist down. He called out to the others not to follow him. They could hear he was down below the road level but it was so dark that they had to borrow a motorbike from a neighbour so they could shine the lights down to find him."

RIGHT Fr Leo's mother, Kitty, shares a few words with her son after his ordination in All Hallows College, Drumcondra, on June 14th, 1959. Fr Leo's friends and family had fought hard for permission from the Vatican for his ordination, including having a frame built which enabled him to say mass in a standing position

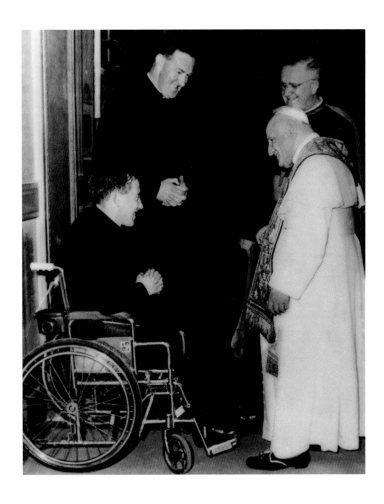

ABOVE Fr Leo was given a private audience with Pope John XXIII in Rome in 1960, during which the Pope gave Fr Leo's friend, Fr Brendan O'Sullivan (pictured behind Fr Leo), or 'Big Brennie' as he was widely known, a second nickname, 'Padre Alto'

Leo was brought to the local hospital in Moulin, where he stayed for a night before being transferred to Clermont-Ferrand to undergo an operation on his spine. Brendan and his father flew out to visit him, and Brendan stayed on for a few weeks so that he could accompany Leo on the journey home.

In Ireland, Leo was admitted to the Richmond Hospital in North Brunswick Street. Bernie remembers visiting him there on his twenty-third birthday. "The nursing care in the Richmond was excellent but with hindsight it was a pity they didn't fly him straight from France to Stoke Mandeville, because they had to get a specialist from Stoke Mandeville to fly over to assess him and put him on the waiting list."

After a few months, Leo was transferred to Stoke Mandeville to begin intensive rehabilitation. Brendan visited him there. "It was tough at first. The staff would leave his dinner on a table, where he couldn't reach it. That was one of the ways they taught him to transfer into his chair and help himself. They placed a great emphasis on the importance of upper body strength and León would spend hours going along uphill stretches of corridor." Bernie adds: "It was amazing how much León achieved in six months at Stoke. I was shocked at the change in him when he came back. He was full of ambition and determined to go on with his studies. But of course, no one had ever been ordained in a wheelchair."

The Bishop of Dunedin, Dr JP Kavanagh, and the President of All Hallows, Fr William Purcell, were both supportive of Leo's request to resume his studies in 1957. Normally, seminarians lived on campus, but an exception was made to enable him to live at home. Leo's mother helped him get ready in the mornings and Brendan helped him into the car. During the day, he was assisted by his classmates, including his close friend Brendan O'Sullivan, who at 6ft 6in was nicknamed 'Big Brennie'.

Leo was very close to his mother, although he liked to affectionately poke fun at her respectability. IWA member Anne Ebbs remembers hearing a story about a visit from Bishop Conway, who was a friend of Leo's father. "Leo's mother put out the best table cloth and the best cutlery, and when Bishop Conway sat down, Leo winked at him and said, 'Mother, where did we get all this stuff from?' She was mortified and chastised him later, but he told her it served her right for having airs and graces!"

The most significant support for Leo's ordination came from the upper echelons of the Church. Brendan remembers: "My father asked Bishop Conway to put in a good word for León in Rome. Conway joked, 'You don't need me. You have the number one, McQuaid, on side!'" John Charles McQuaid, Archbishop of Dublin, had links with Leo's father through Blackrock College and he had indicated his support for the ordination. "McQuaid was very influential in Rome but it still took a lot of convincing. They wanted to know strange details about León's accident, like whether he had lost consciousness in his fall. León also had to prove that he could stand to say mass, so a cousin of my mother's, Michael Quinlan, who worked in the Richmond, managed to get a standing frame made. The frame consisted of a base that poles locked into, and then León would wear callipers and a belt with rings that looped over the poles."

Through the support of Bishop Conway and Archbishop McQuaid, Leo received a special dispensation from the newly elected Pope John XXIII, allowing him to be ordained on June 14th, 1959. "McQuaid understood the significance of the occasion and insisted on doing Leo's ordination himself," says Brendan. McQuaid also offered him a post in the Dublin diocese, but Brendan says he turned down the post because he felt he had committed himself to Dunedin and that "there must have been a reason for him to go there".

Fr Leo decided to undertake a BA in UCD, in preparation for a role as head of religious education in Dunedin. Lectures and classes were held on the top floor of the UCD building in Earlsfort Terrace, and he relied on a group of classmates to carry him up. Fr Paul Freeney, a close friend of Fr Leo's, says, "We take it for granted now that wheelchair users are in airports, cinemas, stadiums and colleges, but it's important to remember that Fr Leo was one of the first. Leo and I went to every cinema in Dublin trying to find places that were suitable. He would go to all the games at Croke Park, where he sat on his own at the bottom of Hill 16. He was such a regular that Mícheál Ó hEithir would often start his commentary by saying, 'There's Fr Leo Close sitting in Hill 16…' Leo opened up those doors for wheelchair users, simply because he loved sport and wanted to enjoy it."

In 1960, Fr Leo captained the Irish team to the first Paralympic Games in Rome, where he competed in archery, table tennis, javelin and shot-putt. He was received in Rome as a minor celebrity and offered a private audience with Pope John XXIII. One Italian newspaper, *Orizzonti*, requested special permission to photograph Fr Leo practising archery and saying mass. The article reads: "Fr Leo showed courtesy in every way, graciously allowing a photographer to be present while he said mass in the private chapel of St Patrick's Irish Church in Rome. This is the story of a wonderful priest [...] who doesn't view life negatively and doesn't get depressed about his situation. Whatever happens, he smiles and jokes [...] because his faith is strong and he is happy to have the privilege of being a priest."

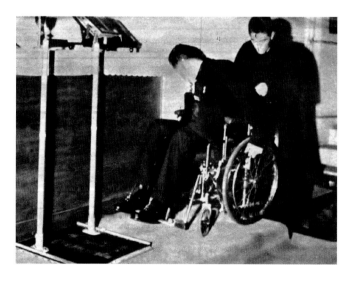 

ABOVE In pictures taken by Italian newspaper, *Orizzonti*, in September 1960, at St Patrick's Irish Church in Rome, Fr Leo is shown being assisted onto the altar beside his standing frame, and then saying mass using the frame. A few years after his ordination, Fr Leo received permission from Rome to say mass in his wheelchair

When Fr Leo returned from Rome, having met and talked to athletes from other countries, he was determined to establish an organisation to support wheelchair users in Ireland. It was as a result of Fr Leo's energy that on November 10th, 1960, the meeting took place in the Mater Hospital which led to the founding of IWA. "He realised that people in wheelchairs were hidden away behind closed doors and had no say in anything," says Bernie. "He believed we had to do something about this. León had a big heart and an innate ability to get things done for people. He had gone out and found Jack Kerrigan, Oliver Murphy and the others, and had got them involved in the paralympics and then in IWA. In the early days, our whole family became involved in IWA. My mother and I used to collect patients from the Royal Hospital for the Incurables in Donnybrook to work on flag days. There would be about thirty people in total, and we would be stationed in a caravan at the bottom of Grafton Street, supplying fundraisers with sandwiches and cups of tea. León would always be there for the counting of the money, and it was those flag days that kept IWA going for a long time."

"He had a very ready smile, and was unable to sit still for long, and he was a heavy smoker, which made him a very human priest"

Fr Leo continued his studies, undertaking a Diploma in Higher Education in 1962 at UCD, and finally an MA in Catechetics at the Lumen Vitae Institute in Brussels in 1963. As the first Chairman of IWA, he influenced many of the early strategic decisions made by the Association, including the acquisition of the site for IWA's headquarters in Clontarf, in partnership with his friend Lady Valerie Goulding. Fr Leo later explained that the person selling the site would only sell it to a Catholic, so he had to buy the land in his name and then sell a portion to Lady Goulding so that she could build the Central Remedial Clinic.

In the summer of 1964, the time came for Fr Leo to leave Ireland for Dunedin. Fr Freeney accompanied him on part of the journey. "We flew Dublin, New York, Chicago, Nebraska, Los Angeles – and then he went on to Tokyo for the Paralympics before going to New Zealand. He had lots of people and places he wanted to see along the way. We were guests of Mayor John F Collins of Boston. Mayor Collins was in a wheelchair himself, after contracting polio in the fifties, and he was delighted to meet Leo. In Washington, we visited the White House where we met one of the late President Kennedy's aides, and I remember taking Leo step by step up to the top of the Lincoln Memorial, so that he could see the location of the great political and civil rights rallies."

Fr Leo then went on to Tokyo for his last Paralympics as part of the Irish team. Teammate Oliver Murphy remembers: "After the games, the Irish team accompanied Fr Leo on his trip to Tokyo airport, singing Irish songs all the way." At subsequent Paralympics, in Tel Aviv, Israel, in 1968 and Heidelberg, Germany, in 1972, Fr Leo competed as part of the New Zealand team, although the games always provided a welcome opportunity to catch up with old IWA friends from home.

In Dunedin, Fr Leo took up his position as head of religious education, and also established an organisation to support wheelchair users. "The Wheelchair Association in New Zealand had a strong emphasis on sports," says Bernie, who moved out to New Zealand a few years later. "He became well known in New Zealand because he presented many television programmes. One of the programmes consisted of short sermons or homilies based on his memories or thoughts, and he also presented a programme where he played recordings of Irish music." In 1972, Fr Leo was awarded an OBE in New Zealand for his work with wheelchair users.

Despite his success, Fr Leo missed home. He remained good friends with Jack Kerrigan and Oliver Murphy, and came home periodically for long visits. "It was always wonderful to have him back," says Brendan. "There were so many people he wanted to see and who wanted to see him. He'd buy a car for his holidays and drive around the country. Jack Kerrigan's

LEFT Fr Leo captained the Irish team at the first Paralympic Games in 1960. He is pictured with teammate Joan Horan, who won gold medals in archery and swimming at the Games, as they are welcomed by Robert Briscoe, Deputy Lord Mayor of Dublin, at Dublin Airport on their return from Rome. Leo Close senior is standing behind Fr Leo

wife, Rosemary, remembers Fr Leo coming to visit them in their cottage. "I can see him sitting in our kitchen. He had a very ready smile, and was unable to sit still for long, and he was a heavy smoker, which made him a very human priest. Although he'd had to fight hard to be ordained, he had no exalted opinion of himself. He loved a good practical joke and wasn't a saintly type. He admitted that he was lonely and sometimes wished that priests could marry so that he could have the benefits of companionship that he saw in my relationship with Jack, and in Oliver's relationship with Joan." Brendan acknowledges that Fr Leo was liberal on many issues: "He might not have said it from the pulpit, but in the confidence of friends, he spoke his mind."

"When I'd have a drink with him," recalls Brendan, "he used to say, 'If I get into my fifties, I'll be doing well'. He knew the pressure on his kidneys and the lack of exercise would reduce his life expectancy." By the time of Fr Leo's last visit to Ireland in 1976, he was beginning to show signs of ill health and a few months later he was diagnosed with advanced liver cancer. Brendan left his young family in Ireland to spend Christmas with Fr Leo when he was dying. "When I got to Auckland, I couldn't get a flight to Dunedin. I was told it could be days before a flight became available. But then the man heard my name and said, 'Are you anything to Fr Leo Close?' When I said I was his brother, he told me he'd get me on the first flight."

Brendan was with Fr Leo when Jack Kerrigan came to visit him a couple of weeks before he died. "It was very moving when Jack arrived to see him – the fact that he had gone to so much trouble to get there." Jack was able to update Fr Leo on all the news from home, including the progress of IWA. Brendan reflects, "León lived for wheelchair users. He helped everybody he could, and never used the collar to wield power. You always met the person, rather than the priest."

Fr Freeney is keen to see Fr Leo's achievements recognised. "He was a very broad-minded man and he blazed a trail for other wheelchair users. The Irish Wheelchair Association owes its existence to him and when I see the many wheelchairs in Croke Park, Landsdowne Road, and on our city streets, with their lively active occupants, I remember the long years when Leo was a solitary figure at sports events and many other functions, and I know he left his mark on Ireland."

Based on interviews with Bernie Grant, Brendan Close, Fr Paul Freeney, Rosemary Kerrigan, Oliver Murphy, Greg Harkin and Anne Ebbs.

Jack Kerrigan

An intelligent, compassionate man who spoke openly about his experiences

1928 - 1994

In June 1949, twenty-one-year-old Jack Kerrigan dived from a bridge in Fife, Scotland, into the river below. Although he was an experienced diver, who had regularly dived off Rogey Rock into the Atlantic near his home in Bundoran, he lacked experience of rivers and dived with no appreciation of the current's strength. The impact was catastrophic, causing an instant compression fracture to his spinal vertebrae. Jack's friends waded in and dragged him out, leaving him on the banks of the river while they went back to the work camp where they were staying to raise the alarm.

Jack later recalled that it felt as if he had been cut in half. "When it happened to me," he wrote, "my first reaction was puzzlement. What has happened? What exactly is wrong? Why am I lying like this? I try to turn over, but nothing happens. I try again; it seems I cannot get my legs into gear. A dreadful thought occurs: perhaps they are not there? Gingerly, I put a hand down [...] and find that I have legs alright. My hands can feel my legs but my legs don't feel my hands."

Jack, who had been working as a carpenter on a dam-building project, was taken to the Bridge of Earn Hospital in Perthshire. Staff immediately sent for his parents, and by the time his father arrived from Ireland, Jack had been diagnosed as having permanent paralysis from the chest down, and had also developed pneumonia. Jack later told his wife, Rosemary, that he remembered the ward sister standing beside his bed, telling his father that he was going to die. "Jack could hear this, and while every breath was a struggle, he was thinking, 'I'm not going to die, I'm not going to die'. His father was so convinced that he would die that he left the hospital and went to order a coffin. The undertaker, on hearing Jack was not actually dead, gave his father a business card and said, 'He may not die. Come back when he's dead.'"

Years later, Jack's father used to say, "That undertaker was a lot smarter than the doctors in the Bridge of Earn." Jack survived the pneumonia, but bleak prognoses became a regular theme in his life. After fifteen months in the Bridge of Earn Hospital, Jack returned to his family home in Bundoran on a stretcher, and his parents

ABOVE Jack being carried onto an aeroplane in 1960

were told, "Make everything as comfortable as possible as the kidneys or the sores will kill him within a year." This time, they refused to believe the doctors and set about nursing him. "My overdue demise became a family joke," Jack later wrote. Rosemary attributes Jack's survival to the incredible care he received at home. "When he came home he didn't know how to look after himself, he didn't know that he should drink plenty of water, and he was so desperately thin that his brother Paddy joked, 'Tie a bigger knot in your tie, it'll hold your head up.' But Mrs Kerrigan was fantastic and they had an excellent Jubilee Nurse. Between them they cured most of his sores and built up his strength through good home cooking."

Jack's family encouraged him to meet up with his old friends. "My social rehabilitation was pressed on by the family and in no time my bedroom had become a gambling casino with poker predominating and tea and buns about ten o'clock every night. I often quarrelled with my family about their 'show him to everybody' attitude. This sometimes resulted in heavy going for me, as I was a sitting duck for the religious zealots and cure peddlers. Had I been in a position to dictate, I think I would have shied away from people at this time." But Jack's family persisted. His brother, Paddy, bought him his first wheelchair and Jack began to journey to neighbouring houses or to the parish hall for theatre and musicals. One evening, Mrs Kerrigan connived with a good friend of Jack's to get him to the local dance hall. She got him to put on a clean shirt and tie, telling him that he was going to the pub, but as soon as they were out the door, Jack was pushed down to the ballroom. Jack later recalled, "The first dance I ever attended in a wheelchair was entirely against my own will. I had been very fond of ballroom dancing, and I thought it would be sad for me and embarrassing for the girls I used to dance with if

"Either I am content to be the family invalid [...] or I take responsibility for myself and lead a normal life within the confines of a wheelchair"

I were to appear, like a skeleton at a feast." But his friend refused to listen. "His argument was that if I was going to die young, I might as well see what I would be missing." Eventually Jack surprised himself by "enjoying the night immensely". After that night, Jack went out more often, and began to enjoy socialising again. He was appointed chairman of the local table tennis club and although he couldn't attend most of the matches, the team members would always call in to him on their way home, and Mrs Kerrigan would make tea while they discussed the results.

In the holiday season, Mrs Kerrigan ran a boarding house, and to accommodate guests, the whole family – Jack included – moved out to a big shed at the back of the house. After a few years, the Kerrigans extended their house so that Jack could run a sweet shop from the house in the summer months, providing him with some income of his own. Life improved for Jack but he still struggled with daily tasks. He writes of "peaks of enjoyment" and "troughs of despair" during this period. He yearned for greater independence. "Either I am content to be the family invalid, given regular meals, weekly trips to the pub, mollycoddled and cocooned by family and friends, shielded from cold and work, until such time as my parents die and I end up in the county home, or I take responsibility for myself and lead a normal life within the confines of a wheelchair."

In July 1959, Jack received a visit from Fr Leo Close. Rosemary recalls, "Leo had been studying at All Hallows with a guy from Bundoran, and after Leo was ordained, he and his friend set out on a holiday around Ireland, staying in convents, as they could in those days, and one day he was brought to see Jack. Apparently, he was only planning on staying for an hour, but he ended up staying the whole day. Jack wasn't terribly well at the time, but Leo gave him so much information and was able to show him a car with hand controls, which Jack was amazed by."

For Jack, this was a life-changing experience. "Leo told me more about spinal injury and how to live with it in that first meeting than I had ever heard before. He was the first person to tell me that activity was the price of life. He gave me a demonstration of how to dress myself, advice on a suitable chair, suitable urinal, how to manage my bowels and much more. He had been rehabilitated in Stoke Mandeville, and we both agreed I must get there quickly."

ABOVE Jack in Bundoran with a friend in the early 1950s

In February 1960, Jack was admitted to Stoke Mandeville Hospital. After a week of tests and investigations, the great rehabilitation pioneer Ludwig Guttmann came to his bedside to tell him that while they could not rehabilitate him, they could certainly help him to rehabilitate himself. In the six months that followed, Jack learnt how to manage daily tasks, underwent physiotherapy, learnt how to swim, and started playing sport.

While Jack was at Stoke Mandeville, his father, who was a railway driver with the Great Northern Railway, was transferred to Drogheda. When Jack returned, he found himself living in the same town as three other young wheelchair users, namely Oliver Murphy, with whom he had become friends at Stoke Mandeville, Jimmy Levins and Joe Craven. Jack's parents had also bought a car, which was fitted with hand controls, and Jack began to learn to drive, allowing him "untold freedom and independence". He began to see Fr Leo regularly and became part of the Irish team for the 1960 Paralympics, which led to his involvement in the foundation of IWA. Jack was one of the ten people who met in the Mater Hospital, Dublin, on November 10th, and voted to establish an association to further the interests of wheelchair users. He was appointed secretary of IWA and took an active role in the running of the Association, working in IWA's pools office in Pearse Street, and boarding on week days in the National Rehabilitation Hospital (NRH).

At that time, Rosemary Burges was working as an occupational therapist (OT) in the NRH. "For months, a patient in the OT Department, Jimmy Garrigan, had been trying to get me to meet Jack. 'Miss Burges, have you met Jack Kerrigan?' he kept asking. One day, Jack was driving out the gateway of the Cedars (NRH) as I was going in. He waved to me, but in those days if a man I didn't know waved at me, I just ignored him. Apparently Jimmy asked Jack later, 'Have you spoken to Miss Burges yet?' and Jack replied, 'No, and I don't want to. She's a complete snob!'

"One day I came to work and Jimmy was in the workshop early, looking very down. 'Jack Kerrigan has been admitted. He's so ill the curtains have been drawn around his bed,' he said." Jack had become gravely ill as a result of a kidney infection, a condition to which he was prone due to the lack of specialised care in the months after his accident. Indeed, long before she met him, Rosemary had heard Jack's case being cited as an example of what could go wrong if a spinal injury wasn't managed properly.

Towards the end of 1961, Rosemary was surprised to receive a referral card for occupational therapy with Jack's name on it. "I went to see him, and Jack said, 'Give me something to do, so I can set an example'. He asked for some leather and started making a safety belt for Joan Horan, one of the other patients, who had difficulty with balance and worried about falling out of her wheelchair." The NRH had metal workshops and woodworking rooms, and as Jack's health improved, he was able to use his carpentry skills to assist the occupational therapists, by making equipment for patients who were leaving and by operating the in-house printing press. One day, Jack offered to go get some supplies, and Rosemary went with him. "It was the first time we were alone, and already there was the beginning of a feeling of interest between us."

Jack and Rosemary's relationship developed from there, but not without resistance from others. "We were pariahs in some respects, and it was hard going. The nuns weren't happy to see staff and patients fraternising, so I left my job and took a position in a Dublin psychiatric hospital. When I went to the chief psychiatrist to ask for a week's leave to get married, he said, 'You know I don't approve of you marrying a paraplegic'." In March 1966, Jack and Rosemary were married by Fr Leo's close friend, Fr Brendan O'Sullivan, near Rosemary's family home in Oxfordshire. They bought a three-roomed cottage on an acre of land in The Ward, Dublin, and in 1970 and 1972, they adopted their two sons, Jonathan and Paul.

Jack worked on various IWA projects, from holidays to branch development, and in 1965 was appointed manager of IWA's workshop in Fairview, where members carried out contract work, such as assembly and packing. He later oversaw the construction of the first IWA building in Clontarf, and for a period in 1967, was the acting chief executive of IWA. Jack represented Ireland at both the 1964 and 1968 Paralympics, where he competed in the table tennis, archery and swimming events. In 1967, he had the dubious honour of being the first paraplegic in Ireland to have a kidney removed, an operation which greatly improved his general health.

In 1977, Jack and Rosemary went to Australia to visit Jack's brother, Paddy. While they were there, Jack travelled to New Zealand to visit his old friend, Fr Leo, who was dying of liver cancer. "Leo appeared unconscious much of the time, but was still alert to what was going on around him and at times joined in lively discussions and had good craic with Jack," says Rosemary. "Leo was in hospital, so Jack slept in Leo's bed. Jack found it all very difficult because he was so fond of Leo."

Soon after their return to Ireland, Jack, who was having

ABOVE Jack and Rosemary at a Christmas dance in Dundalk in 1965

trouble with his shoulders, decided to retire from his job with IWA and move the family to a smallholding in County Leitrim. "Jack had spent childhood summers in Leitrim, on his grandparents' farm, and he wanted to be part of a community and to have mountains and views around him. We couldn't find accessible accommodation so the four of us lived in a 8ft x 30ft cabin, without running water, while the house was built. Jack was fantastic. He managed direct labour and ordered the materials. He also made the window sills and the mantelpieces, and hung the doors. We didn't have the money so we had to do the work ourselves, but it gave us great satisfaction.

"Jack had many interests," says Rosemary. "He loved music and drama, was a member of two agricultural show committees, was involved in Sligo IWA, and was the Scout group leader in Dromahair. He also participated vigorously in the 'Stop the Pylons' campaign and continued to ask for updates on this when he was in hospital during the last few months of his life."

After Jack died, many people approached Rosemary and told her about the ways in which Jack had helped them over the years. One old friend, Stanley Miller, who had been in the NRH in the early 1960s, described how "Jack always had time for the man in the corner," a sentiment echoed by Ronnie Conlon, who said that "Jack found something to talk about with everyone he met, whether it was the dustman or the local TD". Ronnie Conlon was one of many younger people with spinal injuries who got to know Jack through the NRH. Rosemary says, "Jack was in the NRH so often over the years that he had many opportunities to influence people with new spinal injuries. He was always very open about his experiences, good or bad, and about the assistance he required, so staff would say, 'Would you talk to so and so about this or that?'" After Jack died, a member of staff in the NRH told Rosemary how important Jack had been as an "informal, unpaid counsellor [...] – a gentleman with a sense of humour who could be kind and firm at the same time".

Based on an interview with Jack's wife, Rosemary Kerrigan, and on papers and letters provided by Rosemary.

Oliver Murphy

A kind and spiritual man with a lifelong commitment to the Association

Oliver Murphy, who turned seventy-five this year, is the only founder member of the Irish Wheelchair Association alive to celebrate the organisation's 50th anniversary. Oliver grew up in Drogheda, County Louth, where he was educated at the local Christian Brothers school, enjoying GAA, athletics and gymnastics in his free time. After an apprenticeship as an electrician, a twenty-three-year-old Oliver moved to Carlow to work in the Carlow Sugar Factory.

One night in July 1959, Oliver began a late shift. "When I arrived, I found the lime kiln had stopped working. This sixty foot structure ground the limestone that was used in the sugar purification process, and was loaded using a steel bucket and a rope. I climbed as far as I could up the side of the kiln and could see that the bucket wasn't tipping properly. A stone had got jammed between the lip of the bucket and the kiln. I couldn't reach the bucket so I shouted down and one of my colleagues went to get a poker. But I was an athletic young lad, and while he was gone, I got impatient and decided to climb to the top myself. I flicked the jammed stone, causing the bucket to suddenly release. The bucket crashed down on me, hitting me on the spine and knocking me to the floor." Oliver's colleagues found him on the ground. "I was taken on a stretcher into the sick room and a priest was called while we waited on the ambulance." Oliver says that the ambulance men who took him to Waterford Hospital afterwards told him that they thought he was "a gonner at least twice".

"The archery got us out, which was a big step, as a lot of people felt self-conscious and worried that people were looking at them"

In Waterford, the orthopaedic surgeon used a silver plate to bring Oliver's spinal column back into line and confirmed that Oliver had a T10 break, paralysing him from the waist down. Oliver remembers experiencing severe pain from the damaged nerve endings on his spinal cord and acknowledges that the months after his accident were dark times. "I'm not a 'holy Joe' but I do have faith. At the time, I was fairly mad at God, but I knew there was nothing I could do, I had to accept it. So I tried to go with the idea of offering my pain and suffering up to God, as a prayer, and this helped."

In April 1960, Oliver was transferred to Stoke Mandeville in the UK, where he says the physiotherapy was so intense he didn't have time to feel sorry for himself. "The focus was all on rehabilitation, on getting back to life. I remember my physio, Mrs Dorph, a tough Norwegian woman. She'd say, 'No slacking! It's for your own good!'" In their free time, patients were encouraged to keep active. "Archery was a big thing in the UK and we used to compete at pubs and clubs. It's one of those sports where you can compete whether you are in a wheelchair or not. The archery got us out, which was a big step, as a lot of people felt self-conscious and

LEFT Jack Kerrigan and Oliver Murphy standing using callipers in Jack's house in Drogheda. Jack's wife, Rosemary, remembers Oliver's kindness over the years. When Jack and Rosemary got married, they had only two single beds, and it was Oliver who gave Jack the money to buy good timber so that he could make a double bed

LEFT Oliver competing at the Tokyo Paralympics in November 1964

worried that people were looking at them." During his three months at Stoke Mandeville, Oliver also made friends with many of the Irish nurses who were over there to train for the changeover of the old TB Hospital in Dun Laoghaire into the National Rehabilitation Hospital (NRH).

Oliver says Stoke Mandeville taught him a lot. "They were world leaders in rehabilitation and they had the right frame of mind. We were imbued with this spirit, a belief that we could do lots of things." Oliver came home in June 1960 after fifty-one weeks in hospital. He moved into his family home in Drogheda, where his parents made a make-shift bedroom for him downstairs, and he did his best to settle back into normal life. "My younger sister Catherine, who was only nine at the time, was a great handler of the chair and used to bring me into town. And one of the lads in the local cinema would pull me onto the balcony."

"We could see that the other athletes were better equipped and had a better life at home. Fr Leo wanted to know what could be done to improve things here – self-help he called it"

Oliver became good friends with fellow Drogheda resident Jack Kerrigan, whom he had met at Stoke Mandeville, and through Jack, Oliver met Fr Leo Close, who had also been at Stoke Mandeville a few years earlier. Fr Leo was leading Ireland's team for the first Paralympic Games in Rome in 1960, and both Oliver and Jack were selected. When they got to Rome, Oliver says, "The wheelchair users were the stars of the show and this really gave us a lift. I was pleased to come sixth in archery, thanks to my Stoke Mandeville training. And then, on the journey back to Ireland, the team stopped at Lourdes. This gave us another lift and when I got home I felt I was on another level of existence. I'd had one hell of a hoist up and from then on, I never felt moody or down." It was this spirit of optimism and hope, the new-found friendships, and the realisation that in many other countries people with disabilities were living independently, that led members of the Paralympic team to join with other like-minded individuals to found an organisation dedicated to improving the lives of wheelchair users in Ireland. "We could see that the other athletes were better equipped and had a better life at home. Fr Leo wanted to know what could be done to improve things here – self-help he called it – and he was really the driving force behind the foundation of IWA in November 1960."

In the early days of the Association, Oliver says the focus was on getting people out of their houses. "Until then, you didn't really see people in wheelchairs. IWA opened up a whole new world, getting people out for socials every week and bringing them on holidays." Oliver also put his energy into building a more independent life for himself. With compensation from the sugar factory, he was able to build a house, which he still lives in today, and an adjoining electrical workshop. He says that his parents, brothers and sisters, extended family and friends were an invaluable support to him throughout this process. Oliver also bought an adapted car and got back to driving.

As Oliver was driving off after an IWA holiday in Cork in 1964, he slowed to say hello to a young nurse who was walking by with her sister tutor. This nurse, Joan, would eventually become Oliver's wife. Joan liked Oliver instantly and remembered him when she saw him again four years later. "I was coming off night duty at Holles Street Hospital and he was on College Green doing an IWA flag day. I stopped and we chatted, and he said he'd ring me that night and we'd go out. Oliver kept his word, and I remember telling a friend, 'I'm after being out with the man I'm going to marry'." In the years that followed, Oliver continued his sporting career, taking up weight-lifting and basketball, and representing Ireland at the Stoke Mandeville Games and the Paralympics in Tokyo in 1964, Tel Aviv in 1968 and Heidelberg in 1972. Joan and Oliver married in 1971 and, over the next decade, life went well for them, with the arrival of two children, Móna and Thomas, and success in Oliver's electrical business.

Then, in 1980, Oliver suddenly became ill. "It just hit me one Friday evening. I was pushing my chair and my fingers kept sticking to the chair. By the following morning, I couldn't stir, I was like a ten-ton weight. Joan managed to get me down to the Lourdes Hospital, where they gave me a shot of multi-vitamins. But my breathing was getting shallower and soon a helicopter was called to take me to the Richmond Hospital in Dublin. Doctors eventually diagnosed Guillain-Barré syndrome, a rare viral condition that attacks the central nervous system." They were able to stabilise Oliver, although in the weeks that followed, Oliver "couldn't eat, drink, breathe, move or sleep". Oliver was transferred to the NRH where he was placed in a rotating bed. His recovery was slow and when, months later, he was allowed to go home, his muscles were so wasted that he felt like "a bag of spuds". His former paralympic trainer, Raymond Buckley, came by three times a week for over a year to help Oliver in his battle to re-gain strength.

Both Joan and Oliver believe that a positive attitude has enabled them to get through any set-backs they have faced. Joan says, "We have a great life with our children and our granddaughter, Cáit. We have a lot of respect for each other. When the kids were growing up, they used to say, 'This house does not prepare us for life – everything is too calm!' We didn't worry about things like what they wore or what they did with their hair. Móna used to look at Oliver and say, 'Is he for real? How can he always be in such good humour?' After nearly forty years of marriage, Joan knows that he is for real. "I remember when he had Guillain-Barré's and was unable to talk, you could still see in his eyes that he was trying to say thank you to the nurses who helped him." Joan believes that this peacefulness comes from "not having a chip on his shoulder and being a very accepting person". Last summer, Oliver had a triple heart bypass, from which he has recovered well. "I feel very lucky to be able to enjoy time with my family and also to be involved in the 50th anniversary celebrations of an organisation that has been so much part of my life."

In October 2010, Oliver Murphy received an honorary doctorate from the University of Limerick, in recognition of his work to support people with disabilities.

ABOVE Oliver with his wife Joan

Kay Hayes

A stylish and enterprising woman who loved cars and loved life

1929 - 2008

Kay Hayes was born in 1929, the third eldest of twelve children, six girls and six boys, seven of whom are alive today to share their memories of Kay. The family home was an old farmhouse, located a mile down a bóithrín on the banks of the River Boyne in County Meath. Her brothers and sisters recall how they were taught to kneel and say their prayers every morning before being brought to school in a pony and trap.

In the early 1950s, Kay moved to London, where she worked as a hairdresser for a few years before beginning training to become a nurse. In March 1956, Kay and her siblings were brought home by the sad news that their younger brother, Jerome, had died. Jerome was buried on a Thursday; on the Saturday that followed, a gust of wind caught a tree that was being felled for fire wood, crushing and paralysing Kay.

Kay's siblings remember the great pain she suffered as she recuperated in Dublin's Richmond Hospital. Fr Leo Close was at the Richmond at the same time and had a great influence on Kay; she would later write that he taught her "how to cope with wheelchair life and to live as independently as was possible".

After nearly two years in the Richmond, Kay returned to the family home. Kay was a stylish and sociable person, and her brothers and sisters remember how tough it was for her not being able to go to Sunday night dances with the rest of them. She would vent her frustration the morning after by banging on the ceiling with the handle of a brush to wake them up so they could bring her to mass. Kay's life improved dramatically when she got her first car, a fibre glass and canvas three-wheeler. The car was ordered from England and delivered, packed in a big cardboard box, to the nearest town on a train. Kay's brothers remember going down to collect it in a horse and cart. The car had hand controls but no space inside for Kay's wheelchair, which instead had to be strapped to the back of the car by a helper. Kay's first trip out was for her driving test with the local garda inspector. From then on Kay never looked back, eventually moving on to a newer model, this time with space for her wheelchair, and then on to her favourite, a Morris 1100.

In 1961, Kay competed in the table tennis and archery tournaments at the Stoke

Mandeville Games. In the months before the Games, she spent hours practising with the bow against a bale of hay in a shed on the family farm, enrolling her younger brothers as arrow collectors.

Kay devised a series of enterprising schemes which enabled her to earn a living. She learned to crochet ladies' jackets, cushion covers and slippers, which she sold door to door. She also invented her own brand of patchwork carpet, using remnants from the carpet factory in Navan, which she would fit together carefully while sitting on the floor.

ABOVE Kay in her three-wheeler in front of IWA's offices in Pearse Street. The car was purchased for £350, taxed for five shillings and insured for just over £2!

LEFT A serenely glamorous Kay with Nurse Maguire in the Richmond Hospital in 1956, just a few months after her accident

Kay meticulously supervised the building of her own home in the mid-1960s and, later in life, became passionate about the principles of universal design, often taking the time to persuade local businesses to re-think the design of their buildings.

Kay was very proud of her involvement in the foundation of IWA. In her seventies, she wrote a memoir of her early days with the Association. She describes helping to set up the wheelchair pools, raising £37 by doing a house-to-house collection in her three-wheeler, and an early morning collection at the Cattle Market in Dublin after which she had to endure the smell of cow dung on her wheels all the way home – a trial quickly forgotten thanks to the full box of money donated by the farmers. Kay recalls the joy of receiving a red ten shilling note from actor Noel Purcell on a flag day at Santry Stadium: "I must add that even though confined to a wheelchair, I felt ten feet tall that day."

Based on an interview with Kay's Ireland-based siblings, John, Willie, Betty, Agnes, Sheila and the late Margaret, and also on information provided by Anna (UK) and Philip (USA), and on Kay's written memoir 'Memories of My Early Days with the IWA'.

Joe Domican

A positive and resourceful man,
who loved to work with his hands

1932 - 1999

Joe Domican, from Blackhill in County Kildare, was twenty-four years old when he was paralysed in a motorcycle accident on his way home from a local football match. It was 1954, an era in which rehabilitation services were unheard of in Ireland, and Joe was treated in Jervis Street Hospital in Dublin. "Just before I left hospital, I asked them to give it to me straight," Joe told a reporter from the *Leinster Leader* in 1959. "They told me not to be expecting a cure, as for me there was no such thing." Joe was pragmatic from the start: "I had my mind made up for anything. It was hard but I got over it as I sort of expected the worst."

Joe adjusted well to life in a wheelchair despite the lack of professional rehabilitation services. While he was recovering, he undertook a correspondence course for a Diploma in Art and began painting Irish landscapes. Before his accident, Joe had been a blacksmith and when he moved back into the family home, he set about finding other uses for his workshop. He took the first step towards starting a new business, making prototype souvenirs for the tourist market. Joe's nephew, Patrick, who lived across the road, remembers Joe going to Dublin to show some samples to an official from Bord Fáilte. "The official was finicky, pointing out flaws with the design. Joe came home in bad humour and went up to the pub for a few pints. Then the next day he got a phone call from them, placing an order for a couple of hundred of each type. So he was in trouble all of a sudden because he had to make them all!" The souvenirs, which ended up being sold in hotels and

"They told me not to be expecting a cure as, for me, there was no such thing"

shops all across Ireland, were silhouettes made from sheet tin, into which Joe cut and hammered Irish designs. Joe later diversified, making trophies for Mondello Park Racing Circuit as well as chinchilla cages. He also discovered a talent for sign-writing, and was sometimes seen sitting in the bucket of a tractor as he painted signs over shop doors.

Joe was known to have a daredevil streak. "The motorbike accident didn't deter him!" says Patrick. He drove a hand-controlled car which was notoriously unreliable. Patrick remembers one occasion when the hand controls failed while they were descending a steep hill at full speed. Patrick was instructed to dive down to Joe's feet to push the brake with his hands, but it was too late; they drove straight through the open door of a neighbour's garage, flattening a lawnmower against the back wall.

After the National Rehabilitation Hospital (NRH) opened in 1960, Joe spent several months there, learning how to carry out everyday tasks like getting dressed and making tea. Joe's brother, Christy, remembers him coming back with new confidence. "Joe never saw anything as an obstacle, especially the wheelchair," says Christy. "He was real active, always on the go."

Joe's main motivation for getting involved in the establishment of IWA was that he wanted to meet other people in the same situation, and to find out how they managed with various aspects of life. "In the early days, Joe used to get excited just to meet someone else in a wheelchair," says Patrick. One of the first wheelchair users Joe got to know was Jack Kerrigan, and it was most probably Jack who encouraged Joe to drive into Dublin for the inaugural meeting of IWA on November 10th, 1960.

Joe went on IWA holidays to Wexford, Galway and Skerries, and took part in many flag days. He liked to play the accordion or banjo in the back of the IWA bus, with the doors at the back of the bus wide open, and was partial to a hot whiskey after a day of fundraising. Joe maintained links with IWA throughout his life, particularly with his local branch in Athy. When he was in his fifties he met his wife, May Grace, at a local IWA social. May had multiple sclerosis and, as she got older, Joe took on the role of carer.

Joe took great pride in making his home wheelchair accessible. He devised homemade access solutions for all areas of the house, including a wheel-under cooker and a self-supporting sink. He modified everything to ensure he could live and work independently, and visitors from the NRH often came to look at his clever adaptations.

Joe was very much part of his local community. "He never missed mass and used to pick neighbours up on his way in," says Patrick. Joe was a fine musician and throughout his life he played the banjo at local dance halls, hotels and village events. Occasionally, he would be so focused on getting his wheelchair into the car that he would leave his banjo on the side of the road. "He had a few scares," says Patrick, "but everyone knew it was Joe's banjo, and somehow it was always found and returned."

In the early 1960s, Christy remembers the local people organised a fundraiser to send Joe to Lourdes, and when Joe got home he gave a moving speech at a dance in the village of Ardclough "He thanked the people for sending him to Lourdes and he said that he got cured over there because he saw people a lot worse than himself, people who were laid out and unable to use their hands. He said he counted himself lucky because he was able to play music and make a living by his hands."

Based on an interview with Joe's brother, Christy Domican, and his nephew, Patrick Domican.

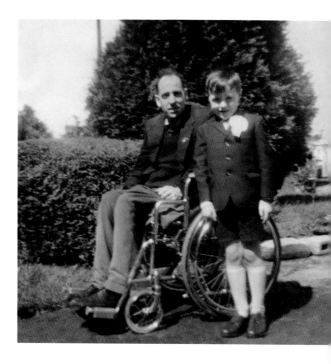

ABOVE Joe with his nephew, Patrick, in 1967. He was a kind uncle and was loved by his nephews and nieces, who remember getting rides on the front of his wheelchair

ABOVE Joe playing the banjo at an event in the local school

Joe Craven

A happy-go-lucky man who loved to meet new people

1910 - 1964

Joe Craven was fifty years old when he attended IWA's inaugural meeting in November 1960. He didn't live to see the fifth anniversary of the Association, but he is fondly remembered by his nephews and nieces, and by fellow founder member, Oliver Murphy.

Joe was brought up in a small redbrick cottage in the north of Drogheda, one of four boys and five girls. He lived at home until he was in his mid-thirties when, after the end of the Second World War, he left Ireland to go to Scotland to work on shipbuilding on the Clyde. In 1950, the scaffolding he was working on was blown away from the side of the ship by a gust of wind, causing him to fall from a height, and paralysing him from the waist down. His hospitalisation and rehabilitation took place in Glasgow, far from his family, although his brother Frank and sister Bridget went over to visit him.

Eventually, Joe received compensation of £5,000 from his employer, as well as a modest pension. He returned to Drogheda to live with his mother. Joe's nephew, Terry Allen, who was a child at the time and lived in the house with them, remembers, "Joe's mother had to mind him. She was fairly old and she had to dress him every morning and get him ready. They were always bickering and calling each other names. 'Bless your ugly face,' Joe would say to her as he left the house. But underneath it all, there was a great bond of affection."

The house was small and, like many houses in the 1950s, it had only an outside toilet, so Joe had to rely on a commode. Terry recalls that Joe used to walk up and down the hallway using callipers and crutches, having been advised by doctors that this would improve kidney function and build his strength. "I couldn't tell you the number of times he used to forget to bar the front door and he'd be doing a turn and I'd come running in and knock him down. I'd run through the house and up the back garden while he cursed me!"

Terry describes Joe as "a fun-loving, happy-go-lucky character who loved life and made the best of what he had".

ABOVE Joe with his mother and his sister, Bridget, in the back garden of their house in Drogheda

Joe loved horse racing and playing cards, and was a fan of Celtic Football Club, arranging to have the Glasgow papers posted over so he could follow the team. He enjoyed music and dancing, never missing the weekly dance at the Abbey Ballroom in Drogheda, where he would sit in the corner and "do a bit of jigging in his chair".

Joe got to know Jack Kerrigan, who had his accident around the same time and who also lived in Drogheda. Terry says, "Jack was friends with singer Ruby Murray, who was like Madonna at that time, and he brought Ruby down here to the house one night. They all sat in the kitchen while she sang hits like 'Heartbeat' and 'Softly, Softly'."

ABOVE Joe and his neighbour, Nancy, in the doorway of the family home

"He said he liked to be out with others in wheelchairs because he didn't feel like he was the only one, and it was good to see other people in that situation making the best of life"

Through Jack, Joe got to know Oliver Murphy and Jimmy Levins, both of whom lived in Drogheda. On the night of November 10th, 1960, Joe's brother-in-law, Pat Lambe, accompanied Joe as he travelled to the Mater Hospital, Dublin, for the meeting that would result in the establishment of IWA. Terry remembers Joe's pride at being part of this special group, and his sense that life was about to improve for wheelchair users like him. In the year that followed, Joe trained regularly with Oliver and Jack, and in 1961 he was part of the Irish team that travelled by plane to the Stoke Mandeville Games in the UK.

Terry believes Joe's main motivation for getting involved in IWA was a desire to meet new people and see new places. "He had good days and bad days, but the Association really took him out of himself and gave him a bit of a lift. He said he liked to be out with others in wheelchairs because he didn't feel like he was the only one, and it was good to see other people in that situation making the best of life."

With his compensation payment, Joe was able to purchase a car with hand controls. Terry remembers him bundling ten or more children into his big blue and white station wagon and bringing them out for a day at the sea in Laytown. Joe also had other luxury items like a radiogram, a collection of hundreds of 78s, and a camera. Any child who made his first communion had to call in to Joe to get his photo taken. Terry says, "All the children loved Joe. Every Christmas, he'd call us in one by one and give us an envelope with Christmas money. The older children got a pound, which was a lot in them days, the younger got ten bob."

As Joe got older, he became renowned for missing doctors' appointments and refusing to exercise. He began to put on a lot of weight, contributing to the failure of his kidneys and his premature death at the age of fifty-four in 1964. His funeral was attended by many of the other founder members, and Fr Leo led the prayers.

Based on an interview with Joe Craven's nephew, Terry Allen.

Jimmy Levins

A gregarious, fun-loving publican

1933 - 1983

Jimmy Levins was born and raised in Congress Avenue on the south side of Drogheda, County Louth, and began his working life in the local Cairnes brewery. In the early 1950s, he met and fell in love with Josie Clarke, a pretty girl whose family was from the north of the town. Josie's brother, Michael, recalls, "They were only a young married couple when they went off to Birmingham, England, to make their fortune, and that's where Jim had his accident. He was working as a roofer on one of the big stadiums – Old Trafford, I think – when he fell and was paralysed."

After his initial hospitalisation in Birmingham, Jimmy was transferred to Stoke Mandeville for rehabilitation. His spinal injury was incomplete, and although this left him with hope of regaining some movement, it also resulted in great pain at times. Michael says, "I remember he'd get these dreadful nerve pains, like an electric shock running through him, and sweat would be pouring down his face while you were talking to him, but then it would pass and he'd continue talking." Josie managed to get a job in the kitchens in Stoke Mandeville so she could be near Jimmy and look after him as much as possible. Jimmy spent several months there, and would possibly have met Fr Leo during this period, before being discharged and returning to Ireland. Both Jimmy and Josie's families were deeply upset by the news of Jimmy's accident. Michael says, "It was a great shock to both families and I'll always remember when Jimmy and Josie finally came home. It was Christmas time and we were all looking forward to it. But I think it was hard for Jimmy and Josie, having to meet people for the first time since the accident and dealing with public perceptions, and on Christmas Day, they just wanted to be alone."

For the first few months, Jimmy and Josie stayed with Jimmy's sister, Eileen Byrne, but eventually Jimmy received a compensation payment from his former employer. "It was big bucks at the time," says Michael, "and they used the money to buy a pub called The Thatch on the Donore Road in Drogheda." Jimmy and Josie ran The Thatch for about six years and became well-known publicans. They had two large dogs, an alsatian and a boxer, and Oliver Murphy, fellow IWA founder member and Drogheda resident, remembers hearing stories about Jimmy getting the dogs to pull his wheelchair along the country roads beside the pub.

Drogheda had a lively music scene, focused around the Abbey Ballroom and the show band circuit, and Jimmy and

ABOVE Jimmy Levins practising javelin with his two nieces

Josie soon began to socialise again. Michael remembers that "Jim was always in there in the midst of it, available for everything. He was a very sociable character and that didn't change after his accident. In fact, he got even better at socialising after he became involved in the pub."

In 1960, Jimmy was selected to compete in the club throwing event at the first Paralympic Games in Rome. It was during the Rome trip that the idea of founding an organisation to support wheelchair users in Ireland was sown and Jimmy would have been involved in the many debates that took place in Rome and on the long journey home. Both Josie and Jimmy attended the meeting in the Pillar Room on November 10th, 1960, at which the IWA was founded. While Jimmy was too busy with the pub to take on a significant role in the day-to-day running of the Association, he and Josie held many fundraising pub quizzes to support IWA's work. Jimmy also kept up his sports training for a couple of years and was part of IWA's team at the Stoke Mandeville Games in 1962.

In the early 1960s, Jimmy and Josie moved to another pub, The Market Bar, on Magdalene Street in the centre of Drogheda. Michael recalls, "The pub was next to a sales yard and all the farmers would be in on market day.

ABOVE Jimmy and his wife, Josie, before Jimmy's accident

There was a real buzz around the place. Jimmy would always be behind the bar with Josie. All sorts of characters would come in, from farmers to solicitors, and there would be betting and great conversations." Michael says that Jimmy enjoyed a drink. "He was a bar-stool philosopher, an intelligent man who could talk on any subject. And he was a great lad at funerals and weddings – singing and talking, and always the centre of attention." The Market Bar was a two-storey building – unlike The Thatch, which had been a cottage – so Jimmy had to devise various solutions to access problems, including a platform lift to the first floor which operated on a pulley system. "It was a crude affair," says Michael. "Jimmy would go out to the back of the building and roll into this box frame, which was suspended on a chain. By pulling the chain, he could hoist himself upstairs."

Oliver Murphy remembers Jimmy's ongoing battle with pain. "He suffered with what we call 'root pains' or phantom pains, and I think he found it hard to cope at times. He tried various medicines and drugs, and even had an alcohol block inserted in his spinal column to try to block the messages, but it didn't work. When he was on the tablets he felt like a zombie, and I think having a drink was the only thing that helped him cope with the pain."

Jimmy and Josie retired from the pub trade in the 1970s and moved to College Rise in Drogheda. "Jimmy was often sick," says Michael, "but Josie seemed to be able to cope with him. He'd get very ill and then somehow Josie would revive him." Despite his frequent ill health, Jimmy's death at the age of forty-nine was unexpected. Michael believes Josie missed Jimmy and his fun-loving approach to life greatly. Oliver Murphy says Jimmy and Josie seemed to have a very close relationship. "Jimmy was a gas character, a very nice person and good fun to be around, and you couldn't meet a nicer lady than Josie."

Based on interviews with Josie's brother, Michael Clarke, and Oliver Murphy.

Fr Paddy Lewis

Committed to improving life for people with disabilities

1935 - 2001

Fr Paddy Lewis, while not a founder member of IWA, was present at the Pillar Room meeting on November 10th, 1960, and was strongly in favour of the establishment of the Association. As a student member of the Holy Ghost Order, he was unable to add his vote to the other eight votes without permission from the Order, which could not be obtained at such short notice. Later in the decade, he took an active role in the running of the Association and he had a formative influence on areas of policy and organisational structure.

Fr Paddy was born in Sandymount, Dublin, in 1935. His father, Colonel Jack Lewis, is remembered for repeatedly leading the Irish Show Jumping Team to victory in the international arena, and Fr Paddy inherited a love of horses. As a boy, he attended Blackrock College, run by the Holy Ghost Fathers, where he was a good student and sportsman. In 1954, he entered the seminary of the Holy Ghost Fathers at Kimmage Manor, Dublin. It was there, during his second year of studies, that he contracted polio and became a wheelchair user. He was hospitalised first in Cherry Orchard Hospital and then in the Mater Hospital, which is where he met Fr Leo Close and became involved in the Pillar Room meeting. On leaving the Mater, he convalesced at Kimmage Manor, before returning to his studies and becoming the first wheelchair user to be ordained as a Holy Ghost Father in 1964.

In January 1964, Fr Paddy became Honorary Secretary of IWA, a role he held until 1969 when he became Chairman for four years. During this period, he studied for a degree in social science at UCD, and also became Chairman of IWA's Social Services Committee, encouraging IWA to engage more social workers and occupational therapists to work with members in their homes. Fr Paddy had learnt to drive in the early 1960s, and he understood the importance of driving for mobility and independence. He was involved in the establishment of IWA's driving school, and argued for the use of standard vehicles rather than three-wheeled cars, which he regarded as unsuitable and stigmatising. He also played a role in IWA's campaign, which began in the late 1960s, for duty-free petrol, the remission of road tax and the removal of VAT on new vehicles.

In 1970, he was responsible for the introduction of a democratic constitution for the Association. Fr Paddy had a deeply held belief that the Association should listen to its members and respond with appropriate services. He was widely regarded as a capable administrator. Former IWA Board member and volunteer Phelim O'Reilly describes him as "a man of purpose and perseverance", someone who "would not take no for an answer when he believed he was right".

In 1974, Fr Paddy left Ireland for the United States, studying for a Master's degree in social work in Missouri, and later becoming a counsellor with diocesan charities in the area. In 1981, he transferred to San Francisco, where he worked on a programme for the integration of people with disabilities into the community. Reflecting on Fr Paddy's life, Phelim O'Reilly says, "Throughout his life, he remained devoted to improving life for people with disabilities and those living in poverty."

Based on a profile of Fr Paddy by Marion Henry, published in IWA's magazine, Push, in Oct/Nov 1969, and on an obituary of Fr Paddy by Phelim O'Reilly, published in the Sunday Independent on October 21st, 2001.

Joe Davis

A founder member IWA has failed to trace

Joe Davis was a patient in the Mater Hospital when he attended the meeting which resulted in the establishment of IWA on November 10th, 1960. Little is known of Joe, although a souvenir booklet produced in 1968 to commemorate the opening of IWA's new building in Clontarf, Dublin, states that he was deceased at that point in time. The booklet also says that he became a wheelchair user as the result of a fall down stairs. IWA would be interested to learn more about Joe Davis, so that we can better acknowledge his contribution in the future. It is our hope that someone reading this book will know more about him and will contact the Association.

BELOW A letter from Sir Ludwig Guttmann to Fr Leo Close, congratulating him on the foundation of IWA

NATIONAL SPINAL INJURIES CENTRE

(ROYAL BUCKINGHAMSHIRE & ASSOCIATED HOSPITALS MANAGEMENT COMMITTEE)

TELEPHONE :
AYLESBURY 5050

REPLY SHOULD BE ADDRESSED
TO THE DIRECTOR

PATRON

THE COUNTESS MOUNTBATTEN OF BURMA,
C.I., G.B.E., D.C.V.O., LL.D.

STOKE MANDEVILLE HOSPITAL
MANDEVILLE ROAD
AYLESBURY
BUCKS

18th November, 1960

My dear Leo,

    I was delighted to learn from Jack Kerrigan that you have formed an Irish Wheel-chair Association, with you as the Chairman and he as the Secretary, and I am writing to send you my warmest congratulations on this achievement. I hope the Association will develop, under your leadership, and no doubt, in due course, this will be another feather in your cap.

    I have written to tell Jack that I am delighted and honoured to accept patronage of your Association, and if I can be of any help I shall be only too pleased.

    With kindest regards to you and all my other friends in Ireland.

        Yours sincerely,

Sir Ludwig Guttmann

Irish paralympic team members discuss the possibility of setting up an organisation to support wheelchair users, Rome, 1960

Irish Wheelchair Association in the

1960s

LEFT **Members of the first Irish Paralympic Team, Jack Kerrigan, Fr Leo Close, Joan Horan, Oliver Murphy and Jimmy Levins, along with team support staff, as they board the Irish Airlines flight to Rome in September 1960. Picture courtesy of** *The Irish Times* ABOVE **Founder members Fr Leo Close and Jack Kerrigan in conversation in the National Rehabilitation Hospital, where much of the early planning for the Association was undertaken** BELOW LEFT **Oliver Murphy presents Miss Pauline Carroll, Cavan, with a cheque for £125, her winnings in the IWA Pools**

1960   **1961**   **1962**

SEPTEMBER 1960
The first Paralympic Games

The first Paralympic Games were held in Rome in September 1960. Wheelchair users from twenty-three countries competed in the games, including a team of five athletes from Ireland: Jack Kerrigan, Fr Leo Close, Joan Horan, Oliver Murphy and Jimmy Levins. The Irish team came twelfth on the medals table, returning with a great sense of pride at having competed for Ireland. The Irish athletes also came home energised and inspired by their conversations with athletes from other countries, many of whom were living independently. They realised wheelchair users in Ireland deserved more out of life and became determined to change things at home.

NOVEMBER 1960
The foundation of the Irish Wheelchair Association

On November 10th, 1960, four members of the Irish Paralympic team came together with some other progressive individuals in the Pillar Room of the Mater Hospital, Dublin, and formed the Irish Wheelchair Association. The founder members came from different parts of the country and different professional

backgrounds, but they were all driven by one objective: to improve the lives of wheelchair users living in Ireland.

APRIL 1961
Establishment of the IWA Pools

The Irish Wheelchair Association Committee soon realised that if the Association was to meet its goals, which included the establishment of hostel-style accommodation for members, it would need a steady stream of income from fundraising initiatives. The first such initiative was the Irish Wheelchair Association Pools, a betting system based on the weekly football results from the English Football League. The

National Rehabilitation Hospital supported the establishment of the pools by providing temporary office space and allowing founder members Jack Kerrigan and Kay Hayes to stay on in hospital accommodation after they had completed their rehabilitation in order to work on the pools. The income from the pools was vital and by the end of 1961, IWA had rented its first premises at 171 Pearse Street, Dublin 2. The Pearse Street office became a hive of fundraising activity, from the pools to flag days and annual sales of work.

JANUARY 1962
IWA sets criteria for membership

In 1962, an organised Board of Management replaced the old management committee. The Association had also established a constitution which stated: "That confinement to a wheelchair would automatically qualify a person to membership, but that applications from persons suffering from other physical disabilities should be considered on their merits." 'Associated membership' was also introduced to ensure that volunteers would have a voice in the Association.

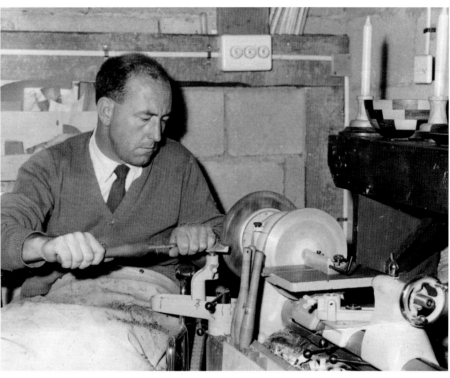

ABOVE **IWA member Miriam McSharry working as a secretary in the Clontarf headquarters** RIGHT **Workshop Manager Jack Kerrigan, 1965** BELOW **Sir Ludwig Guttmann, founder of the Paralympics, speaking at the Tokyo Paralympic Games in 1964**

1963　　　　　　　　　　　　　1964

AUGUST 1963
Medical social worker appointed
The needs of the membership were the main concern of the Board and in order to address members' issues on a one-to-one basis, the Association took the big step of employing a medical social worker in August 1963. The role of this social worker was to visit members at home, handling requests for assistance and also ensuring that the work programme for the Association reflected members' needs.

OCTOBER 1963
Agreement to purchase Clontarf site
In October 1963, Lady Valerie Goulding of the Central Remedial Clinic and Fr Leo Close agreed to jointly purchase eight acres of land in Clontarf, Dublin. The sale wasn't formalised until 1965 when the Association paid £9,940 for its 4.5 acre share.

JULY 1964
First IWA holiday held in Cork
Cork was the venue for the first IWA holiday in the summer of 1964. The holiday was a resounding success and the annual holiday programme went on to become one of the most valuable initiatives developed by IWA for its

members. Holidays were held in schools during the summer, with beds set up in classrooms, and halls used for dining and socials. For many participants, an IWA holiday was their first break away from the family home or institution in which they had been raised. A team of volunteers, including students from All Hallows College, ran the holidays, and many friendships were formed amongst members and volunteers.

Local communities also became involved in the organisation of the holidays and, in this way, holidays led to the development of IWA branches around the country.

NOVEMBER 1964
Second Paralympic Games in Tokyo
The second Paralympic Games took place in Tokyo in November 1964. Once again, Ireland sent a team of five athletes, which included Fr Leo Close, Oliver Murphy and Jack Kerrigan. The team performed well, but the event was also tinged with sadness because when the games were over Fr Leo had to depart for New Zealand to take up his role in the parish of Dunedin. Oliver Murphy remembers the whole team travelling to the airport with Fr Leo, singing traditional songs all the way.

FEBRUARY 1965
Opening of the Marino workshop
In February 1965, a second property was rented in Marino in Dublin to cater for the needs of the Industrial Therapy Scheme, more widely known as the IWA workshop. The workshop was managed by Jack Kerrigan and provided space for members to take on contracts for assembly and packing work.

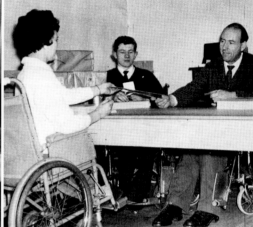

LEFT **Members, volunteers and musicians (believed to be members of Emmet Spiceland, including Donal Lunny) having a sing-song after an IWA social** ABOVE **Workshop Manager Jack Kerrigan with two participants preparing collection boxes for flag days in 1966** BELOW **An IWA holiday in Galway, 1966**

1965   **1966**   **1967**

JULY 1965
Weekly IWA socials get going
In the summer of 1965, member Paddy Crookes set about organising weekly socials in Dublin. Suitable halls were hired, volunteer drivers were recruited and the Legion of Mary was enlisted to serve tea and biscuits. The entertainment was provided by up-and-coming local bands. The IWA socials became the highlight of the week for many members; one member told Paddy Crookes that he had not been out of his home for three years before the socials started.

MAY 1966
Flag day at Nelson's Pillar
Regular flag days were held throughout the 1960s, usually in Dublin City Centre. Groups of members and volunteers would congregate on College Green or O'Connell Street, and at the end of the day, they would reward themselves with a cup of tea in Bewleys. Several volunteers recall a memorable flag day in May 1966, two months after the bombing of Nelson's Pillar, when they set up a collection point on O'Connell Street beside what was left of the pillar. In a covert early morning operation, the volunteers hoisted a theatre dummy, dressed

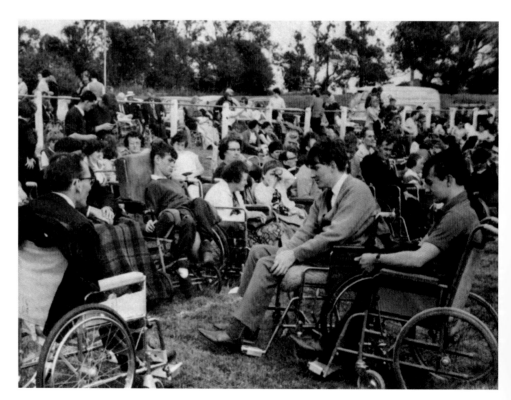

LEFT **Driving school instructors, students and vehicles, 1969**
ABOVE **Member Rosaleen Gallagher and President de Valera share a cup of tea during an IWA holiday in St Paul's College, Raheny, while founder members Jack Kerrigan and Oliver Murphy look on** BELOW **A telegram with well wishes on the opening of the Clontarf headquarters from Fr Leo in New Zealand**

1968   **1969**

as Nelson and strapped into a wheelchair, to the top of the remaining portion of the pillar. The prank succeeded in drawing the attention of passers-by to the collectors below and they went home with full buckets.

MAY 1967
Construction of Clontarf headquarters
Construction work began on the site IWA had acquired for its headquarters in May 1967. Early plans for the site had focused around the idea of a purpose-built hostel for members, but by the time building work could begin, this concept had been replaced by plans for an assembly hall and offices. These buildings would cater for the workshop and the social and sporting activities that had by then become so popular.

It took a few months for a prefabricated, cedar-clad building to be erected and by September the centre was being used for sports on Wednesday nights and socials on Thursdays. By November 1967, the pools staff from Pearse Street and the workshop participants from Marino had relocated to Clontarf. The centre also became home to the Association's administration and expanding social services team.

MAY 1968
Official opening of Clontarf headquarters
Áras Chúchulainn, as the headquarters in Clontarf would be named, was officially opened on May 20th, 1968, by the Minister for Health Seán Flanagan. Over three hundred people attended the opening and the occasion received newspaper and radio coverage. Fr Leo, now settled in New Zealand, sent his good wishes in a telegram to be read at the opening.

JUNE 1968
Introduction of tax relief for drivers with disabilities
In June 1968 Charles Haughey, then Minister of Finance, introduced the Disabled Drivers and Disabled Passengers (Tax Concessions) Regulations. This important piece of legislation outlined the rights and entitlements of drivers with disabilities. By the end of the decade, a variety of tax breaks, including a VAT/VRT relief scheme, fuel rebates and local authority grants were on stream to aid people with disabilities with vehicle purchase.

JULY 1968
De Valera visits members on IWA holiday
IWA was holding two holidays a year by 1968, catering for approximately a hundred wheelchair users and fifty volunteers. In July 1968, members on the Dublin holiday at St Paul's College, Raheny, received a visit from President Éamon de Valera. De Valera took time to chat with individual members, many of whom were from remote rural parishes, and Jack Kerrigan later recalled being astonished by de Valera's ability to speak of people he knew in every person's home parish.

NOVEMBER 1968
Paralymic Games in Tel Aviv
The third Paralympic Games took place in Tel Aviv, Israel. A team of seven athletes travelled to the games, returning with nine medals.

Mary Meenaghan

Raised six children in the West of Ireland with no support services

Eighty-three-year-old Mary Meenaghan has been living with multiple sclerosis (MS) for over fifty years. These days she attends her local IWA Resource Centre in Belmullet, County Mayo, three days a week and enjoys day trips and holidays with other members. But Mary remembers a time when life for people with disabilities in the West was very different. "In the fifties and sixties, there were very few people with disabilities around here and there were no support services at all. We had absolutely nothing but people's good will."

Mary was brought up in Fallaugh, Belmullet, and married her husband, Martin, in 1951. "We met at a wedding. He was from one part of town and I was from the other. Nowadays everybody mixes, but we didn't mix back then." In the late 1950s, when Mary was pregnant with her fourth child, she began to experience unusual symptoms. "My leg was so heavy. I had no pain, but I couldn't run around the way I was used to. I went to the doctor and he sent me off to Dublin for tests. They did everything: looking in, up, down. Eventually they told me I had 'disseminated sclerosis' – that's what they called multiple sclerosis in those days. 'It won't kill you,' the doctor said, 'but you are in it for the long haul.'"

> *"Fr Leo. I knew him. He came in to see me in the Richmond.*
> *He was so nice. He was an angel. 'Come on,' he said, 'you're only very*
> *young. Always look up, don't look down.' He was sorry for me,*
> *I could tell – and I'd only four children then!"*

Mary travelled to Dublin for further tests in 1961 and again in 1963. "I was up in the Richmond Hospital. I remember when I came up in 1961 there was talk in the hospital about a new organisation to help people with disabilities, and on my next visit, some Legion of Mary people came to my bed and talked to me about becoming a member of IWA."

Fr Leo Close regularly visited the Richmond around that time, and when Mary is asked whether she met him, she clasps her hand to her face and falls silent for a minute. "Ah," she sighs, "Fr Leo. I knew him. He came in to see me in the Richmond. He was so nice. He was an angel. 'Come on,' he said, 'you're only very young. Always look up, don't look down.' He was sorry for me, I could tell – and I'd only four children then! Poor Fr Leo, Lord have mercy on him. He'd be an inspiration for anyone. 'Nothing in the world wrong with me,' he used to say about himself. There was something about him. He got you talking and it was always good talk. Anyone who could talk to him for five minutes would wish to be with him always. Oh, I often wondered what happened to him..."

With four children and little money, Mary had no choice but to adapt to her limited mobility and get on with family life. "Two more children came along in the early sixties," says Mary. "And four of my six were delivered at home. 'Ah, come on, come on!' the midwife would say when the baby started to come. That's the way it was!" The family lived in a farmhouse in the countryside, just outside Belmullet. "We had our own cows and would make our own butter. There was no cooker or heating. I used to bake the bread in the hearth. We'd a kitchen-cum-sitting room with a big table where I'd sit to do everything. I'd wash the baby in a basin on the table, peel the potatoes, do everything there.

"Nobody came to help. Martin was the only one who helped me. Ah, what an amazing man he is. One in a million. I was lucky.

"This began to change in the late 1970s, when an IWA volunteer started organising days out for the few local people with disabilities"

ABOVE Mary drinking a mug of holy water at St Derbhile's Well, a holy site which she and other members of IWA's Resource Centre in Belmullet visit regularly

He was so good when the children were growing up. And he worked so hard, cutting the turf and selling it, and working on the roads. We had nothing and I think some people thought there was shame in our situation, but I didn't mind people talking about me. I did my own thing. It was hard for the children though, poor things. Each day, I had a big list of things they had to help me with – getting the water, and the turf to heat the place. I had no choice but, God love them, they missed out."

In the mid-1960s, Mary's sister, who had emigrated to America, came home to visit. "She brought me my first wheelchair, all the way from Chicago. I think it cost her about ten shillings. I remember it had solid wheels." The small kindnesses of family and neighbours were for many years the only support that Mary received. This began to change in the late 1970s, when an IWA volunteer started organising days out for the few local people with disabilities. "There was no IWA centre at the time, but there was a very good girl called Anna May Leech. She used to pick us up from our homes and bring us out in her car. We'd go to different people's houses for a cup of tea. By then, my balance was gone and it was very hard for me to get out. What she did really meant something. I often think of it now."

In 1992, IWA began a home visitation service to support Mary and other people with disabilities living in the area. This led to the opening in 1996 of an IWA Resource and Outreach Centre in Belmullet, which Mary has been attending ever since. Staff at the centre often ask Mary to speak to younger people who have been diagnosed with multiple sclerosis. "I don't mind if they talk to me," says Mary. "One girl used to phone me every single day. It's a real problem, this disease. It has struck people in so many different ways. Just lately my speech is going. When I talk to my daughter on the phone, she says, 'Don't worry, Mam, it's grand,' but I know myself."

Mary refuses to take any medication. "I've never taken any tablets, not a single one. I don't believe in them." Instead, over the years, she says she has taken comfort in seven pilgrimages to Lourdes, many of which were organised by IWA, and regular trips to Knock. She also likes to visit St Derbhile's Well, a holy site near her home, where she and other members often stop to take a cup of holy water. Mary says she doesn't like to fuss and she has never been a worrier. "I've lived with this disease for over fifty years and I've learnt you have to get on with it and look at the best."

Mary and Martin will celebrate their sixtieth wedding anniversary next year. They have six children and five grandchildren, many of whom live locally. Unfortunately no photographs survive of Mary and her family in the 1960s.

In October 2010, building work started on a new Resource and Outreach Centre, located in Logmore, Belmullet, County Mayo. The centre will provide services such as accessible transport, sports, training, education and social outings for members.

ABOVE Mary with IWA member and volunteer Stephen Meenaghan (no relation), and staff members Catherine Carlon and Rose Coyle

ABOVE Mary being brought up the mountain by her IWA friends, towards the sculpture which is known as 'Derbhile's Twist' or Falmór-an Fód Dubh

Mrs Jessie Dowling

A committed volunteer and fundraiser

Ninety-year-old Mrs Jessie Dowling was a volunteer in the early years of IWA, when life for people with disabilities was very different from today. "Now people with disabilities are independent; they have their own transport and their own lives," she says. "But back then, just the opportunity to get out and meet other people meant an awful lot."

Mrs Dowling got involved through the Ladies Committee in Drumcondra – of which Fr Leo's mother, Kitty, and sister, Bernie, were also members – and quickly became a dedicated fundraiser. She soon branched out from the committee, building up her own network of volunteer drivers, most of whom were off-duty gardaí, to bring members to Croke Park or on day trips to places like Skerries and Glendalough. These trips got many members out of the city for the first time and Mrs Dowling chuckles as she recalls one member's terror at coming face to face with a staring sheep whilst sight-seeing in the Wicklow Hills. Occasionally, Mrs Dowling would bring members to Comhaltas sessions in a favourite haunt of hers, The Warrenstown Arms in Co Meath, where she fondly remembers Fr Leo singing 'Courtin' in the Kitchen'.

Once the weekly IWA socials got going, they became the centre of a lively music scene. Each week, IWA member Paddy Crookes, who had founded the socials with the help of his sister Breda, would organise a mix of traditional music and up-and-coming pop groups – something for all ages. Volunteer drivers would collect members from their family homes or sometimes from residential homes like the Cheshire Home in Donnybrook, and drive them up to Clontarf for the evening. "Some people had wonderful families but others were in difficult or unhappy situations," Mrs Dowling remembers. "I became friends with lots of them and they would tell me things they wouldn't tell anyone." The opportunity to get out every week changed lives and many friendships and romances began. "I could tell you plenty of stories but you might be shocked," she adds half-jokingly.

With no State funding available, fundraising was a huge part of IWA life. As well as getting involved in flag days, Mrs Dowling regularly approached Dubliners for donations for the

LEFT A member of Emmet Spiceland in coversation with Bernie Grant (nee Close), Danny Whooley and Esther Delaney after an IWA social

sales of work, which would be held each year before Christmas in the CIÉ Hall on Marlborough Street. She recalls that those who had least, gave most. "The poor streets in Dublin were so nice; each year they'd have a parcel waiting for me. Francis Street, and round the Coombe – all those little shopkeepers were my friends. I loved them. You know, I would get better presents for the sales of work from them than from the big men." Moore Street shopkeepers and traders were also generous. Every year, on the morning of the sale of work, Mrs Dowling would set off down the street with a strong volunteer, collecting "legs of lamb, milk and roasts" to bring back for the wheel of fortune at the sale. "I never remember anyone saying no – people were very sympathetic to wheelchair users. The little things meant a lot."

"'Ah!' said I, 'I just haven't the neck – I'm also begging for something, and you're only after opening up!'"

On another occasion, Mrs Dowling remembers getting up early and walking to Pearse Street in search of donations. "I went into this man's shop. I can still see him. Ahead of me, there was a nun and she was looking for money for a society and he was giving her some. And the next customer was looking for something for a raffle. So, I went to go out, but the shopkeeper called after me, 'Come here, what was it?' 'Ah!' said I, 'I just haven't the neck – I'm also begging for something, and you're only after opening up!' 'Come back here', he said, 'I'll find you something.'" Mrs Dowling smiles and shakes her head: "He'd great good humour that man!"

Not everyone was so kind. One evening, after a busy flag day, Mrs Dowling and some other volunteers, wheelchair users among them, went into a pub on the corner of O'Connell Bridge. "T'was half a crown to get in and the barman said, 'Excuse me, are they [pointing to the wheelchair users] with you?' I said, 'Yes they are.' And he said, 'Well, you can't come in here.' It was the first time I'd ever met discrimination. 'Why?' I asked. 'They take up too much room,' said he. 'But there's tons of room!' said I. 'No, we don't allow people in wheelchairs in here,' he insisted. 'Well,' said I, 'I hope that you can always walk!'"

Fortunately, such incidents were rare, and Mrs Dowling says many local patrons "would go out of their way to welcome people who were disabled". In particular, she recalls the Parkside Hotel by the Phoenix Park, where the friendly owners would invite members to Christmas dinner each year.

There was great camaraderie amongst volunteers and members as they put their minds to endless fundraising schemes. In spring 1966, soon after Nelson's Pillar was blown up, one volunteer, who had been a manager at the Gaiety, got hold of a theatre dummy. The volunteers dressed the dummy up as Lord Nelson, put him in a wheelchair and, early one morning when the streets were quiet, hoisted him up to the top of what was left of the pillar. The Wheelchair Nelson remained there for the day, drawing the attention of passers-by to the fundraisers shaking their buckets below.

Mrs Dowling remembers that after a hard day's fundraising, she'd drop the bags of money into IWA's ramshackle offices in Pearse Street, where her colleagues Paddy Saunders and Danny Whooley would count it. Mrs Dowling was very fond of them both. "Danny used to play tricks on me sometimes and Paddy would never let on. I remember, one day, the postman brought me a parcel and in it were some knickers with one leg and a bra with one cup, with a note saying, 'These are some articles for your forthcoming sale of work.'" She laughs. "It was all friendship and fun. It's a great thing to work and be friends."

This light-hearted spirit continued after IWA acquired its office in Clontarf in the late 1960s. Mrs Dowling remembers well-known disability campaigner Liam Maguire sitting in the corner of the Clontarf office one day when "two awfully grand ladies arrived in. 'We'd like to help the poor invalids,' they announced. 'We're so sorry for the invalids.' I kept a straight face but Liam was laughing. He told them they were in the wrong place as there were no invalids there. They went off anyway. They were the sort of ladies you'd read about. They meant well but I couldn't see them dirtying their hands. Not the sort of volunteers we wanted!"

Jessie Dowling is originally from County Laois but has lived in Drumcondra for over sixty years. She remains friends with many of the people she met through IWA, including founder member Oliver Murphy and his wife, Joan. It is perhaps fitting that Johnny O'Sullivan, one of the members whom she used to bring to the socials in the 1960s, now collects her every week and brings her to a Comhaltas session at a pub in County Meath.

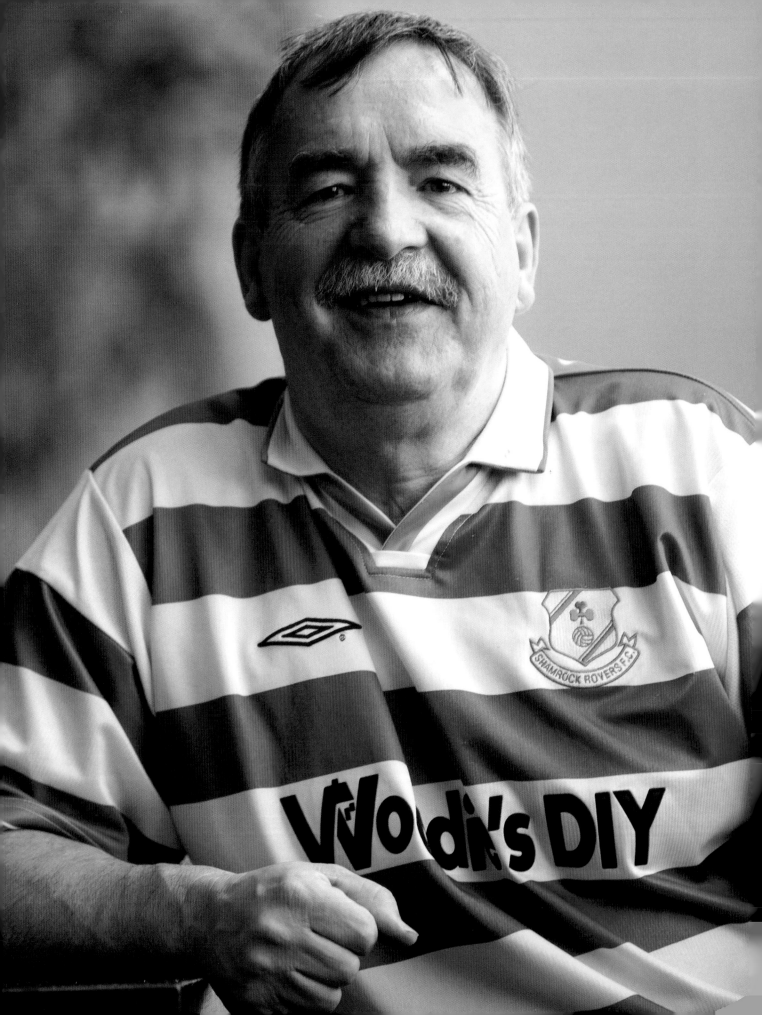

Francis Genockey

Involved in the weekly socials, holidays and the wheelchair workshop

Francis Genockey was born in 1947 in Dublin's Liberties, one of a family of twelve children. "My father was a news vendor. He had a place selling papers on the corner of Westmoreland Street and O'Connell Street. In those days it was one of the best stands. He'd sell Irish and English newspapers. He did that all his life. We moved from the Liberties to Artane when I was young. I don't remember ever being hard up but my mother always said I'd dressed myself since I was eleven years of age. I used to do a paper round in the mornings and when I was a few years older I would sell papers on Saturday nights in the pubs." Francis left school when he was fourteen and took an apprenticeship in a veneer factory in Artane. "I was going to be a saw doctor, working with furniture veneers like rosewood and mahogany. But on December 27th, 1962, when I was fifteen years of age, I had a machinery accident and one of my legs had to be amputated."

Following the accident, Francis remained in Jervis Street Hospital for five or six months, while doctors worked to save his remaining leg, before being transferred to the National Rehabilitation Hospital (NRH) in Dun Laoghaire. "I remember feeling really down in Jervis Street. Just before my accident I had joined Belgrove Football Team in Clontarf and all I could think of was the end of my football career. But when I moved to the NRH in June of '63 I started to come round. When you are there, you see lots of people worse than you and for some reason it cheers you up."

"They didn't care what went on, just as long as they got out!"

Francis was to spend nearly four years in the NRH, during which time he got to know the place well. "I was upstairs on the second floor with the 'amps'. Downstairs on the ground floor you had the paraplegics and the middle floor was for people who had finished their rehabilitation but were coming back with pressure sores and the like. "There were lots of workshops, but I knew I was going back to my old job so I didn't do basket weaving and that kind of stuff. Instead, I concentrated on physiotherapy and started playing table tennis."

Patients were encouraged to go home every weekend, but many of them chose to stay in the hospital. "After a while a lot of us didn't go home because we'd lost touch with our old friends and our new friends were in the hospital. And when you went home, your bed was usually upstairs and you had the hassle of crawling up the staircase." Being in the NRH was about more than just physical rehabilitation and Francis says that he did a lot of growing up during his years there. "Over the years, I came out of myself. I think that happens. Sharing a ward was a big social thing. You'd be in the ward for breakfast and tea and you'd get friendly with the nurses and assistant nurses, and you'd learn from the older fellows. You'd feel yourself getting popular and the shyness would get knocked out of you. I became great friends with two other patients, the late Christy Kelly from Meath and John Mangan from Donegal, and the three of us used to go out to see Shamrock

Rovers play at the old stadium in Milltown." Francis fondly remembers many other characters from his time in the NRH, including Sister Marie, nurses Stella Lambert and Brid Murphy, and fellow patients such as Jack Kerrigan and Liam Maguire.

When Francis was discharged from the NRH in 1966, he went back to his family home in Artane and the weekly IWA socials became the centre of his social life. "In the early years, before the Clontarf building, the socials would be held every Thursday in the Legion of Mary Hall behind St Peter's Church in Phibsborough. I would be picked up by my volunteer driver, who was a Garda superintendent. The social was the main feature of the week and I remember if my driver let me down I'd be in bad form for three or four days. We used to have lots of big entertainers before they were well known, like Emmet Spiceland and the Horslips. The socials weren't only for young people, but the older people never complained about all the loud music. I think they were afraid that if they said anything they wouldn't get picked up the following week! They didn't care what went on, just as long as they got out!"

Less than a year after his return, Francis's job at the factory came to an end when the factory went into liquidation. With time on his hands, Francis started volunteering in IWA. "I got to know Paddy Saunders through the socials and he'd say, 'Why don't you come and give us a hand at the weekend?' And a gang of us would set off in the bus to do fundraising collections around the country. We'd end up at places like the Rose of Tralee. It was great to get away."

Once the Clontarf building opened, Francis started doing assembly work in the IWA workshop. "We'd do all sorts of work. I remember making flags and banners. And in 1969, we got a few bob for making hats saying, 'Back Jack!' for Jack Lynch's election campaign." Francis also began learning how to drive. "It was before the IWA driving school was established but I'd seen people like Jack Kerrigan and Fr Paddy Lewis driving so I realised I could do it myself. In 1969, I bought a blue Austin 1100 and had hand controls put on it in McMeels Garage in South Gloucester Street. Paddy Saunders gave me a few lessons here and there." By the end of the decade, Francis was driving to the weekly socials himself. He had also started to help out with the organisation of the socials, together with fellow members Rosaleen Gallagher and Johnny O'Sullivan. One night, one of the member's daughters, Carol King, came along with her friend Marguerite, a young nurse from Temple Street. "Marguerite and I got chatting and I remember saying to Carol, 'I'll drop Marguerite home'. And things went from there!" Francis and Marguerite married in 1975. "I was one of an awful lot of members who ended up getting married through the socials."

Francis also became a very good table tennis player and started competing in the Leinster League with contemporaries such as Michael Cunningham, David O'Hara and later, Gerry O'Rourke. Frustratingly, he couldn't qualify for the Paralympics due to the nature of his disability. At that time, there was a category for amputees standing up and a category for paraplegics in wheelchairs, but he was not eligible for either. Francis would have to wait until the 1984 Paralympics, when the introduction of a new category called 'Les Autres' enabled him to finally compete and bring back a silver medal.

In 1970 Francis became one of IWA's first employees when he was taken on to set up a specific wheelchair workshop to repair members' wheelchairs. "I think the idea came from one of the members, Fred Keogh. Fred wanted to start up a

ABOVE Francis with a group of volunteers who cycled from Carrick-on-Shannon to Dublin in 1976. Their effort added over £1,000 to the members' holiday fund

RIGHT Francis at work in the wheelchair workshop

repair workshop because at that time it was taking up to three weeks to get a wheelchair fixed by a commercial company. Some companies wouldn't even provide a loan of a wheelchair while the repair was being done, leaving people housebound for weeks on end.

"We'd do the repairs more quickly and make sure no one was ever left without a wheelchair. This made a big difference. People like Liam Maguire would ring up and say, 'I've a problem with my chair, I'm on my way.' And when he arrived, we'd do the repair on the spot while he waited in his car. We also started doing repairs around the country. We had this little mobile workshop – we used to call it 'Ernie', after Benny Hill's song the 'The Fastest Milkman in the West'! We'd bring the van to the IWA holidays so that members could get their chairs serviced while they were there. Simple ideas like that improved life for a lot of people."

Francis worked in the wheelchair repair workshop for over thirty years, after which he became a full-time fundraiser for IWA. Francis and Marguerite live in Julianstown, County Meath. They have three sons and eight grandchildren.

Kathleen Reynolds (nee Egan)

A spirited and determined woman who forged her own path

Kathleen Reynolds was one of hundreds of children with disabilities to grow up in St Mary's Hospital, Baldoyle, County Dublin. Kathleen arrived in Baldoyle in April 1953 when she was just four days old. She never knew her family, although she was once told that her mother was from Offaly. "Because I had nobody, a couple, the O'Briens, used to come in to see me. We got on well and I would look out for them. They had two girls and a boy of their own, and would bring me to their house on Christmas Day and on my birthday."

The O'Briens were one of several local families who would regularly visit Baldoyle in the 1960s, sometimes taking a particular child under their wing. While this contact was generally a positive thing, it could also lead to disappointment. Kathleen recalls: "The day of my communion was the worst day. I've always remembered it. I was only seven or eight, and I was standing there with my splints and crutches, in my white dress, waiting for the O'Briens. I kept looking out the window, thinking 'They'll come, they'll come'. But they didn't come." Kathleen found out afterwards that the O'Briens hadn't been told about her communion. Kathleen also got to know a pilot from Lufthansa who would visit the home. "I called him 'my pilot'. 'Here's my pilot!' I'd shout when he arrived. He'd always ask for me and bring me sweets, a teddy bear or a ball."

The children at Baldoyle lived by strict rules and routines. Kathleen remembers: "You would get up, have your breakfast, go to school, come back for your dinner, and then go back to school until 3pm. When we were young, we used to be in bed early, maybe by 4.30 or 5pm. We all slept in a big ward and the light would be left on. That's why, even now, I always have a light on at night." In the hour or two before bed, Kathleen says she used to get up to "all sorts". "There was a big stairwell next to the lifts and I would sit on the floor at the bottom and throw my ball up the stairs and then catch it when it came back down. Me and the ball was the best thing! I spent hours doing that."

Kathleen also remembers the excitement of getting her first proper wheelchair. "My very first time to get a

LEFT Kathleen with baby Michael, of whom she became very fond during her time in Baldoyle

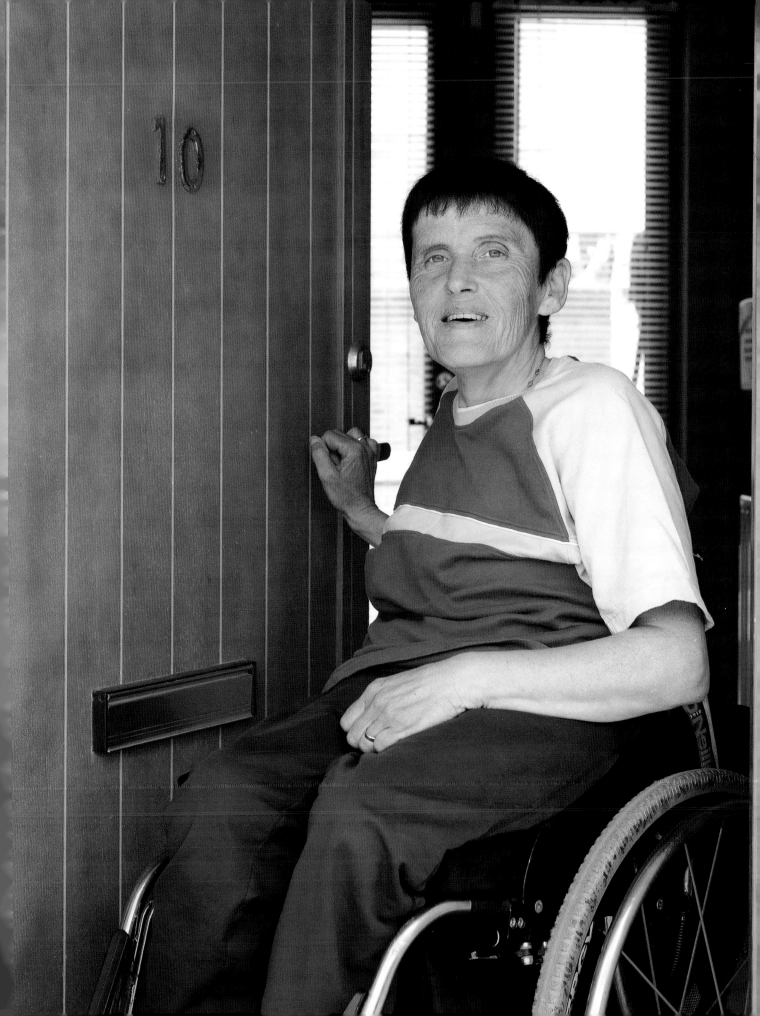

ABOVE Kathleen's team photograph for the 1976 Paralympics in Toronto

wheelchair with big wheels was when I was nine or ten. I thought, 'Now I'm going to belt up and down the yard for ages!'" Kathleen was so rough with her chair that both wheels fell off and she had to crawl up and down the yard looking for the missing nuts to put it back together. Kathleen's wheelchair came to symbolise freedom from the splints and crutches the doctors pushed her to wear. "When I was up on my splints I'd get sores on the tops of my legs and they'd take two or three weeks to heal. And then one day, a physio burnt my leg. She put me under the heat lamp and went off to have her dinner. It was meant to be for ten minutes, but she left me much longer. I was so badly burnt that it took over a year to heal. I used to have big arguments with the doctors. I'd say, 'You know I'm never going to walk! Why bother putting me through torture?' But things were different then. You had to go by what they said. I remember we were brought into O'Connell Street one day by the matron, and a passer-by accidentally kicked my crutches from under me and I went flying. And, well, I called him all the names under the sun! I used to get so angry and frustrated. The crutches were wasting my time and energy."

In contrast, Kathleen's wheelchair gave her the opportunity to play sport. By the time she was twelve, she was playing table tennis twice a day with her friends in Baldoyle, Michael Cunningham and Martin Naughton. "I call them my 'brothers' because they taught me so much." Kathleen also joined the IWA junior sports league and started training regularly in the new IWA building in Clontarf. In 1969, Kathleen was selected by IWA to represent Ireland at the Stoke Mandeville Games, the first of many international competitions in which she would compete.

The rules at Baldoyle relaxed as the children got older. Kathleen remembers the exhilaration of blasting out records in the hall in the evenings. She also remembers going on her first IWA holiday to Limerick when she was fourteen. "Paddy Saunders came and collected me from Baldoyle in the IWA bus. He had to sign a form saying if anything happened he was responsible. It was just great! A lady called Mrs O'Sullivan – 'Mrs O' as she was known – ran the holidays and she really looked after you. You'd get up, have breakfast, and then go out on the bus exploring. And there was none of this safety strapping business on the bus! There was great freedom in those days!"

Although Kathleen still got into trouble from time to time, she began to get on better with the nuns in Baldoyle as she got older. "They got to understand me and knew I was determined to do what I wanted. By the time I was thirteen or fourteen, they would ask me to help feed the kids and babies every night. I got fond of one little boy, Michael. He'd an intellectual disability. He couldn't understand what was going on and he'd get into trouble with the nuns and then come running after me so no one would hit him! I sort of looked after him."

Kathleen's time in Baldoyle came to an end in 1969 when she turned sixteen and was automatically sent to the Barrett Cheshire Home on Baggot Street. "The day I left Baldoyle, they gave me my crutches and splints and as soon as I was in the taxi I broke them up with my hands and gave them to the taxi driver to get rid of!"

A few years later, Kathleen was transferred to the Cara Cheshire Home in the Phoenix Park. It was there that she met her future husband and became pregnant with her first child. At that point, Kathleen moved to a flat in a two-storey house in Clondalkin with her husband, living independently for the first time in her life. "When I left the Cheshire Home, I knew how to boil a kettle – that was it. I had no life skills. I didn't even know how to start a fire." But Kathleen adjusted to domestic life and went on to raise three sons. "There was a bit of hassle with my first son. People thought I wouldn't be able to manage, but by the time I had my second child, they knew I could cope. I was careful to go to the Health Board with every issue, to look for advice and guidance."

In the days before public transport accessibility, Kathleen would often be seen crawling on to Dublin buses, with two of her boys walking beside her and another strapped to her chest. "I didn't panic. By the time he was five or six, my eldest lad would fold my chair for me and the other lad would put his hands up so that someone could lift him on."

"I often wonder, if I hadn't taken up sports, where would I be now?"

Throughout the 1970s, Kathleen kept up her involvement in IWA sport, competing at many international games including the Paralympics in 1972, 1976 and 1980. She then took a break when her children were young, before resuming competitive table tennis nearly twenty years later, and going on to win countless international medals. "I was determined to go back to what I loved. Even when things are not going well, I never give up hope," says Kathleen. Looking back, Kathleen believes her involvement in sport kept her out of serious trouble when she was growing up. "I often wonder, if I hadn't taken up sport, where would I be now?"

Kathleen is also philosophical about her upbringing in Baldoyle. "I remember when I was a teenager one of the ladies who worked in Baldoyle told me she had tried to adopt me when I was little. She told me how the ladies used to fight over who would do my hair. It might sound strange but looking back I thank God she didn't adopt me. If she had, I might have been mollycoddled and restricted in different ways. I might not be the person I am today. I might even still be in a home. There are two sides to every story. That's the way I think about it."

Kathleen separated from her husband in the late 1980s and now lives in an adapted house in West Dublin, close to her three sons and three grandchildren. She continues to compete internationally in table tennis and also works as a referee.

A standard 1970s-style manual wheelchair, an electric scooter and one of the driving school's Minis, outside IWA Headquarters in Clontarf

Irish Wheelchair Association in the
1970s

LEFT **IWA members John Twomey and John Whelan highlight the inaccessibility of the Courthouse in Cork**
ABOVE **Lord Dunraven with founding member Kay Hayes at an IWA Christmas Party** BELOW LEFT **Celebrated athlete Michael Cunningham at the Stoke Mandeville Games, wearing the traditional white hat worn by all competing male athletes**

1970   1971   1972

FEBRUARY 1970
The establishment of IWA's driving school
In February 1970, the Association set up a driving school which specialised in teaching wheelchair users how to drive using vehicle adaptations. The service was run by volunteers until 1972, when Micheál Saunders was appointed as the school's first driving instructor, a post he would hold until his retirement nearly forty years later. This professionalisation of the service reflected the increasing demand from members. Learning to drive offered members independence and freedom, as well as an opportunity to seek employment, further their education and lead an active social life.

JULY 1970
Stoke Mandeville Games
IWA was represented at the Stoke Mandeville Games which were held on non-Paralympic years. Exclusive to wheelchair users, the 1970 games were particularly successful for the Irish team with Michael Cunningham winning two gold medals and Kathleen Fagan winning two silver medals and one bronze.

JANUARY 1971
IWA elects its first President
At the 1970 AGM, members approved a new governance structure for the Association, which included a new role – a President of the Association – a National Council and an Executive Committee. Local branches would elect their representatives to the National Council prior to the national AGM. The new role of President was defined 'not as one of executive power, but one of honour, calling for respect and conferring of dignity'. In January 1971, The Right Honourable Lord Dunraven was inaugurated as the first President of the Association. He continued in this role for twenty years, until his retirement in 1990.

JUNE 1971
Access to public buildings
Following a national strategy to advocate for improved access to the built environment, An Foras Forbartha (the National Institute for Physical Planning and Construction Research) agreed that in the future public buildings would be designed so that people in wheelchairs could make full use of all facilities. IWA also joined local authorities in arranging grant aid for such facilities and for adaptations which needed to be made to private homes.

JUNE 1971
Annual holiday in Dublin
IWA's annual holidays continued to provide members with an opportunity to socialise and make friends in a new environment, as well as providing a needed break for carers. In addition, by the early 1970s, many of IWA's newly established branches were also organising local holidays.

Annual holidays remained extremely popular with members. School halls would be transformed into dormitories throughout the summer months, using beds provided by the army or Health Board. The holidays were run by a team of volunteers including members of the local community, secondary school students, and volunteers from An Garda Siochaná.

The location for IWA's national holiday in 1971 was Dublin, with members who had travelled from rural locations staying in St Benildus College, Kilmacud, and St Paul's, Raheny, Dublin.

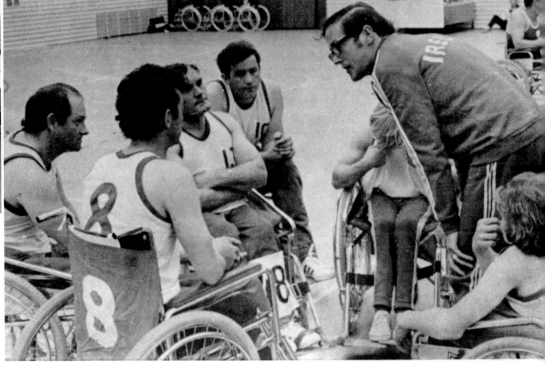

ABOVE **A member and helper enjoying an IWA holiday in Dublin** RIGHT **The Irish Basketball Team of 1972: Oliver Murphy, John Scott, Jimmy Gibson, Harry Ellis, Carl Mulcahy, Michael Cunningham and Johnny Dunleavy, with coach Tony Keane** BELOW **Liam Maguire**

1973   1974

JULY 1972
Heidelberg Paralympic triumph
IWA was represented by a team of thirty athletes at the Paralympic Games in Heidelberg. The Irish team competed in every event at the games, which included archery, swimming, table tennis, basketball and field athletics. The athletes returned with three gold, five silver and three bronze medals. IWA chartered a plane to bring the team and support staff to the games.

FEBRUARY 1974
Grant assistance for vehicle purchase
In February 1974, the Department of Health announced that the criteria under which people with disabilities could receive grants for the purchase or adaptation of motorised transport had been broadened considerably. Tánaiste and Minister for Health Brendan Corish stated that the criteria had been changed in four key areas, namely:
1 Health Boards were asked by the Department to give the maximum grant of £500 for motorised transport to disabled people who were without jobs but could get a job if they had transport. Up to then, people had to have a job before the grant was payable.

2 Health Boards would consider more sympathetically the position of self-employed people who needed a car to continue working, and the position of unemployed disabled people living in extreme isolation.
3 Most significantly, severely handicapped people who were unable to drive were allowed the grant if another person could drive them to and from work.
4 Finally, cars purchased or altered for the disabled were exempted from Value Added Tax.

DECEMBER 1974
Planning of Dublin City
Twenty-four resident associations and community groups including An Taisce, the Inland Waterways Association of Ireland and IWA agreed to set up a co-ordinating committee to advocate for full public participation in the planning of Dublin City.

DECEMBER 1974
Annual meeting highlights need for access
During the 1970s there was a major concentration of effort on the part of IWA on the issues of mobility and access, including the rights of passengers with disabilities to an accessible public transport system.

Liam Maguire, a young activist, created waves in this area, becoming an impassioned and articulate spokesperson on the rights of people with disabilities. In December 1974, Liam, who was at the time Chairman of the Committee on Legislation and Chairman of the Dublin Branch of IWA, stated at the annual meeting of the branch held in the Royal Dublin Society, that he saw little point in securing independence for the disabled when "they were effectively locked out of public buildings".

LEFT **Delegates at a disco during the 3rd Annual Conference on Leisure, Sport and Culture for Disabled Youth, Iran** ABOVE **Harry Ellis, Colm O'Doherty, Anne Ebbs and Liam Maguire at an Aer Lingus access audit with representatives from Aer Lingus. In the background is Aer Lingus's first ambu-lift** RIGHT **Volunteers from the local community, including Gardaí, enjoying one of the annual IWA holidays** BELOW RIGHT **Jimmy Byrne with Rosaleen Gallagher, as she proudly shows one of her medals to President Hillery, July 1979**

1975   1976   1977

SEPTEMBER 1975
International Youth Conference
From September 9th – 21st, 1975, IWA's Paddy Byrne and Pauline Faughnan led an integrated group of ten young participants to represent Ireland at the 3rd International Conference on Leisure, Sport & Culture for Disabled Youth, which took place in Manzariah, Iran. The focus of the conference was to promote integration in the areas of leisure, sporting and cultural activities.

DECEMBER 1975
UN Declaration on the Rights of Disabled Persons
On December 9th, 1975, the General Assembly of the United Nations signed the Declaration on the Rights of Disabled Persons. The declaration stated that, "Disabled persons are entitled to have their special needs taken into consideration at all stages of economic and social planning."

APRIL 1976
Driving school recognition
In the early 1970s the Association had started the assessment process with the National Rehabilitation Board with the aim of having the IWA driving school recognised as an official

training facility, eligible for government and European funding. IWA argued that the process of learning to drive a car with hand controls was an extension of the rehabilitation process and received approval from the NRB in April 1976.

JULY 1976
Paralympic Games in Toronto, Canada
A team of eighteen wheelchair athletes, ten women and eight men, travelled to the fifth Paralympic Games in Toronto, Canada. Over 1,700 athletes from sixty nations competed in the games. The Irish Paralympic team brought home twenty medals, including four gold, nine silver and seven bronze. A civic reception was held in Dublin's Mansion House, at which tributes were paid to Tony Keane, the team manager, and to the coaching and back-up team.

JANUARY 1977
Death of Fr Leo Close
Fr Leo Close, founder member and first Chairman of the Association, passed away in the parish of Dunedin, New Zealand.

APRIL 1977
Launch of *Dimensions of Need* report
In 1976, a survey on the issues facing people

with physical disabilities in Ireland was commissioned by IWA and conducted by researcher Pauline Faughnan. Five areas, namely education, housing, training, employment and residential care, were identified as requiring attention. The report covered demographic characteristics of members, income, housing, access to support services and integration in the local community.

Findings, published in 1977, revealed that almost twenty percent of members had an incomplete primary education, and over one third of this group had received no formal education. The study also revealed that almost a quarter of members lived in the countryside. Pauline Faughnan wrote, "Living in a rural area for any section of the population has implications in terms of employment opportunities, social facilities and general lifestyle pattern. For that section of the population who, by definition, have mobility problems, implications of residence are even more far reaching." As a result of the study, IWA was able to identify three priorities for the Association: to be a provider of services, to create awareness of disability, and to mobilise local community resources to support its membership. In presenting the Government

with hard facts, Dimensions of Need ultimately resulted in improved funding for services.

OCTOBER 1977
Union of Voluntary Organisations for the Handicapped Conference
Following the launch of Dimensions of Need, which was received with interest by disability organisations, Pauline Faughnan was asked to present a paper at the Annual Union of Voluntary Organisations for the Handicapped Conference in Dublin, which had a large international attendance. Also speaking at the conference was Liam Maguire, who was Chairman of IWA from 1977 until 1980. Liam presented a provocative paper titled *A Fair Deal for the Handicapped*, which focused on accessibility, mobility, education, employment, work, training and rehabilitation.

JUNE 1978
Introduction of Mobility Allowance
In April 1978, IWA publicly criticised the then Minister for Health and Social Welfare, Charles Haughey, for his "failure to answer appeals to improve services for the physically handicapped". Two months later, the Government introduced a mobility allowance of £150 a year, which would be provided to people who were 'severely disabled and still living at home'. Charles Haughey commented, "It is intended to apply to people who are unable to walk and who would benefit from occasional trips away from home."

FEBRUARY 1979
Liam Maguire pursues right to be a juror
In a high-profile legal case, initiated in 1979, Liam Maguire pursued his right to be a juror. In February 1979 he had received a summons to attend jury duty at the Four Courts, which he had accepted while requesting confirmation that he would encounter no 'architectural barriers'. The County Registrar replied,

exempting him from jury duty due to the inaccessibility of the court building. Liam refused to accept this exemption and commenced a legal battle with the State. His legal team was prepared to pursue the matter through the Irish courts and the European Court of Human Rights, but the case ultimately fell due to Liam's death in 1983.

JULY 1979
President Hillery meets 1979 Stoke Mandeville team in IWA
The Irish team competed with success at the 1979 International Wheelchair Games in Stoke Mandeville, winning six gold, six silver and eleven bronze medals. On their return they were greeted by President Patrick Hillery at IWA headquarters in Clontarf. President Hillery was introduced to team members by Lord Dunraven and Irish Team Manager Jimmy Byrne.

SEPTEMBER 1979
Mobility International Seminar
In 1979, Dublin hosted the Mobility International Seminar. The seminar highlighted growing awareness of mobility and access issues amongst Irish businesses, in particular Aer Lingus and Doyle Hotels.

Lord Dunraven

A passionate believer in the importance of raising awareness of disability

Lord Dunraven was one of approximately five hundred people, most of whom were children, who contracted poliomyelitis during the Cork epidemic in the summer of 1956. He was at boarding school in Switzerland by the time his symptoms became apparent and remained there for the duration of his illness, benefiting from the medical expertise developed by the Swiss in the aftermath of their own polio epidemics.

Lord Dunraven returned to his family home in Adare, Limerick, in the Christmas of 1957, when he was seventeen years of age. By then a wheelchair user, his perspective on the world had changed dramatically and he began to observe attitudes towards disability in Ireland. He soon realised there were few wheelchair users to be seen in towns and communities. Furthermore, no one seemed to know how many wheelchair users there were in Limerick, or in Ireland for that matter. "The only thing you could do was ring the local health board and ask how many disabled people were on their books and they would say, 'Urh, uhm, well, as far as we know...'. It became clear that a lot of wheelchair users were not registered because they lived at home and didn't require medical attention. They were stuck in their homes and nobody knew about them except their families."

Lord Dunraven was conscious of his comparative good fortune. "I had everything I could have had to make my life better. I had a full-time carer to look after me. He was my arms and legs, and I could go anywhere I wanted." Lord Dunraven decided to join the Polio Fellowship of Ireland and began visiting other wheelchair users in Limerick. "I got what information I could and started visiting people at home, finding out what they needed. I began to see the problems other people in wheelchairs had, and I did my best to help." It quickly became apparent that a wheelchair user's quality of life depended on his or her family circumstances. "There was no such thing as a professional carer. You were looked after by your wife, mother, father or siblings. If you were young and

RIGHT (l to r) Norman Young (Chairman of IWA), Pauline Faughnan, Lord Dunraven and Brendan Corish, Tánaiste, at the launch of IWA's seminal research document *Dimensions of Need* in 1977

ABOVE Lord Dunraven demonstrates the use of a platform lift as President Hillery and Brian Malone look on. By the 1980s, such lifts were being used to provide access solutions to many public buildings

had brothers and sisters, they could help you get out and about. But if you were older and just had parents, you could be left alone all day while they worked."

The establishment of a Limerick branch of IWA in the 1960s began to provide a social outlet for such people. "There was a huge need for a professional organisation," says Lord Dunraven. "I remember two or three people in Limerick who had hardly been outside their front door until the Association started. On one occasion, we gave a film show in Adare Manor and three of the members who came had never seen a film before. This was because, firstly, their families couldn't get them out of the house and, secondly, cinemas were totally inaccessible."

Lord Dunraven believes that the attitudes of the era also played a role in keeping people with disabilities out of the public eye. "I think it had something to do with that awful feeling of guilt of having someone disabled in your home, as if you had sinned and been punished. In the early days, there was a stigma. I remember when I first went out into the public, it was amazing. People looked at me because they hadn't seen a wheelchair before." This lack of awareness permeated all levels of society, as Lord Dunraven recalls. "Government officials had never looked at disability or access. It was a huge learning curve for them and for the general population. I remember when we had our first 'do' down here for the local Limerick branch, I brought the Mayor of Limerick down for the occasion in an attempt to draw his attention to the issue of accessibility. I said, 'Look, these are your people. These are members of your community. What are you going to do about them? This man can't get out of his own house because there are steps. This man can't go along his street because there are no ramps.' I remember he literally ran from the occasion!"

By 1971, Lord Dunraven's activism had caught the attention of IWA's National Council and he was asked by Fr Paddy Lewis to become IWA's first President. It was at his first IWA meeting that Lord Dunraven met Liam Maguire, with whom he was to become great friends. "When we met, Liam, who was very left-wing, looked at me and practically said, 'What's the likes of you doing up here?' And I said, 'Well, I'll do the best I can, but if you want to get rid of me at any stage, just let me know!'" In the years that followed, Lord Dunraven found Liam Maguire to be an inspiring influence. "He was an amazing person. He had vision and the most incredible stamina. Nothing was too much trouble and if anybody got in his way to stop progress, they got a right telling off! When it came to accessibility and the building regulations, Liam thought it was pointless wasting time at a local level. The buck stops at the top, he'd say. Go to the top and change the legislation, that's the only way to get things done. I remember once he brought the press with him as he tried to get into Government Buildings. Of course, there were steps at the door and the next day's headlines read, 'Citizen unable to access Government Buildings'. Liam embarrassed the Government, but by doing so he got results. He was the man who pushed everything.

"Some people didn't agree with his tactics, but I always thought, if it works, use it. Don't forget, the Government was entering a new era in which they had to care for disabled people. We can't really blame them for being slow to respond because they'd never done it before. And then, of course, there was the amount of money involved.

"Local Health Boards would do their best but often IWA had to fill the gaps. If you broke your back, you could be lying in bed for months waiting for a wheelchair, or having to make do with an unsuitable borrowed chair. Our motto was, if somebody needs a wheelchair, we will find one, get them mobile, and worry about the Health Board afterwards. This wasn't easy, because we were providing wheelchairs to men, women and children – all with very different needs – but our staff were wonderful, travelling around Ireland to ensure members got what they needed."

The right wheelchair could make a huge difference to someone's life, as Lord Dunraven discovered when he got his first electric wheelchair. "I was one of the first members to get an electric wheelchair in the late sixties and for someone like me, with limited use of my right arm, it provided complete independence. Electric wheelchairs became the greatest benefit, physically and mentally, to many disabled people. This remains true today, when an electric wheelchair can be operated by a movement as subtle as blowing. Technology is amazing and the seventies were the start of that."

"People realised that they weren't alone and that there was help out there"

Throughout the 1970s, IWA's membership grew. "A lot of it was down to the lifestyle of the human race – motor accidents, sporting accidents, workplace and farming accidents." IWA branches sprung up in communities around Ireland, providing services and fundraising. "Branches made quite certain that local communities became aware of our cause by organising regular raffles and events. In my local branch, for example, we organised a marvellous walk from Limerick to Adare, stopping traffic along the way and collecting money." Many branches began organising their own holidays, and Lord Dunraven recalls that in the summer months there would be three or four branch holidays going on at the same time, at locations all over the country. "The only criterion was that the accommodation was near to a village and an accessible pub!" Lord Dunraven saw first-hand how these holidays changed lives. "Holidays were a vital, vital part of the Association. It was wonderful to give wheelchair users a breath of fresh air and new surroundings, while at the same time giving the carers respite. The joy at being in the company of other wheelchair users was immense. People realised that they weren't alone and that there was help out there."

As the decade went on, branches got their own buses and outings were organised to the increasing number of accessible venues and stadiums. "When Croke Park, Landsdowne Road and the race meetings became accessible, it was a great benefit," says Lord Dunraven.

RIGHT Lord Dunraven's friend Liam Maguire was an inspiring person who fought many high-profile battles in the interests of people with disabilities

"Those were the days before proper access guidelines and I'll never forget the terror of going to a rugby match and being made to sit below the stand, right next to the touchline, with twenty burly fellows looking like they could land on top of me at any minute!"

ABOVE The top table at IWA's AGM in May 1977 (l to r) Fr Lorcan O'Brien, Harry Ellis, Liam Maguire, Phelim O'Reilly, Lord Dunraven, Norman Young, Phil O' Meachair, Pauline Faughnan, Paddy Byrne, Tony Keane and Ronnie Conlon

By the late 1970s, increased awareness of disability was becoming evident in the tourist sector, with hotels introducing accessible bedrooms and bathrooms, and airports and airlines providing specific training to their staff. "In the days before walkways, air travel could be very difficult. Often a couple of strong porters with no training would carry you from the bottom of the steps into your seat. Liam Maguire worked for Aer Lingus and he was the one who started to organise proper attention to the disabled person's requirements in airports and on aeroplanes."

Lord Dunraven travelled to the United States on several occasions and remembers being inspired by the disability movement over there. "America after Vietnam was suddenly faced with a huge number of disabled voters who, through no fault of their own, were suddenly landed on the state, disabled and in wheelchairs. The American Government was forced to act by very strong and very determined citizens who were looking for the right to live a normal life. IWA kept its finger on the international pulse and if we saw anything happening that might be of benefit to our members, we watched and learnt."

In 1976, IWA commissioned a research programme on the needs of its 1,520 members, resulting in the publication of *Dimensions of Need* by Pauline Faughnan in 1977. This was the first significant document to provide statistics on IWA's membership, answering questions such as what type of disability members had, where they lived, how much assistance they required, and whether they worked or had access to education. It revealed that over thirty-five percent of IWA's membership was totally "confined to the house except for infrequent outings by IWA branches and other voluntary groups".

Lord Dunraven believes "this research did a great deal to support IWA's advocacy work and became the first building block towards future legislation to protect the rights of the disabled person".

Another significant tool in raising awareness of disability was the International Year of Disabled Persons in 1981. "IWA members did a marvellous job in highlighting what was needed to improve the lives of wheelchair users. Many gave interviews to newspapers and television, making quite certain that everyone in the country knew about the Year." One of those interviews was given by Lord Dunraven himself, when he appeared on *The Late Late Show* with fellow IWA National Council members Liam Maguire and Brian Malone.

Looking back, Lord Dunraven believes the International Year of Disabled Persons was a turning point. "In my mind, when one compares the seventies and the eighties, there were huge improvements in awareness and practical accessibility. These improvements continued in the decades that followed. I've seen this in my own community. When I first came back from Switzerland, Adare was completely inaccessible, and then gradually the local community became very much aware. Today we have at least three wheelchair users as residents, and welcome many tourists with disabilities each year.

"I've always believed it is all about awareness and education about disability. I am very proud of the change in the lives of wheelchair users over the past fifty years, a change that has been achieved by the dedication and hard work of IWA staff, volunteers and members. My years in IWA were a wonderful experience and when I attended the IWA Annual Conference earlier this year and saw the work of the founder members and the early days continuing, and our objectives being fulfilled, it made me feel very, very happy."

Lord Dunraven was President of IWA from 1971-1990. He continues to support the Association in any way he can, at a local and national level.

ABOVE Lord Dunraven with his driver Noel Ryan on a visit to McKee Barracks in Dublin. The Irish Army was very supportive of IWA, providing beds for holidays and hosting events. Lord Dunraven particularly remembers the annual Christmas party hosted in Sarsfield Barracks in Limerick

ABOVE Pictured at IWA's 30th Anniversary celebrations in November, 1990, the year of Lord Dunraven's retirement from the IWA Presidency, are: (front row, l to r) Harry Ellis, Lady Geraldine, Lord Dunraven, Frank Mulcahy and Marie Mulcahy, and (back row) Lord Mayor of Dublin, Séan Kenny (left), President Mary Robinson (centre) and friends

Anne Ebbs (nee Sinnott)

Involved in the development of sport up to paralympic level

Anne Ebbs contracted polio when she was fourteen months old. "At the time they blamed it on eating tomatoes, but of course it wasn't that." As a result of her illness, Anne started using crutches. "I was fortunate that I didn't require much surgery and was able to attend the local national school in Donore, near Drogheda, unlike many others who did their schooling in hospital. I just mucked in with everyone else. If I fell, I got up again. I was treated the very same." Anne says she benefited from the encouragement of her orthopaedic consultant, Dr De Wytt. "He was a lovely man. He used to call all the children 'honey bunch' or 'sweety pie'. When I left school, he said, 'You'll have to get a job. I think you'd do well on the telephones.'" Dr De Wytt encouraged Anne to enrol in a commercial course in the NRH in Dun Laoghaire in 1962. "I loved every minute, and during that time I got to know many of the founder members of IWA and eventually became a member." Anne successfully completed the course and in 1963 she took up a position as a telephonist clerk in a footwear factory in Drogheda.

In the summer of 1964, Anne was invited on the first IWA holiday, which took place in Montenotte in Cork. "I remember I was one of the few members on the holiday who was working in what they called 'open employment'. I couldn't get time off other than when the factory was shut down for two weeks in the summer, so the way it worked out, I could only go to Cork for a week. I thought, that's grand, I probably won't even want to stay. But we had such a good time! All these young men arrived and they were real friendly and helpful. It turned out they were all the clerical students from All Hallows, who'd got involved through Fr Leo. I think a few went by the wayside after that, but I wasn't to blame! I made lots of great friends on that holiday and as the week was coming to an end, I said, 'I don't want to go home! What am I going to do?' So in the end I wrote to my boss and made an excuse about not being able to get home. I remember my dread on my first day back. But nothing was said all day and I started to think, this is great, I'm getting away with this. But then at 4pm, the secretary called me to the boss's office, and I got the biggest lecture I'd ever had. He said he'd been told I was to get no special treatment, and that's the way it was going to be.

"We were all looking forward to meeting up again the next summer. In the meantime, an IWA social worker had contacted me and asked me about my lifestyle and whether I got an opportunity to get out and socialise. I said I was fine, I was doing everything. And then, when it came to the holiday, I wasn't picked! I didn't understand at the time but afterwards I realised there were a lot more deserving people – people who didn't have an opportunity to socialise the rest of the year."

In 1966, Anne bought a Mini and started learning to drive. "I got hand controls put on it and my brother Donal gave me lessons. He was a good teacher. I remember I'd be driving along, thinking I was doing great, and he'd say, 'See that pole, stop there!'. He taught me that any fool can drive; it's to be able to stop that counts! And that stuck with me over the years. It took a while to get the confidence to go out without him, but once I got going, there was no stopping me. I got involved in IWA committees, the socials and sport." Anne started playing table tennis and in the late 1960s was invited to join IWA's Sports Committee. "It was the biggest mistake they ever made," she jokes. For Anne, this was the beginning of a life-long

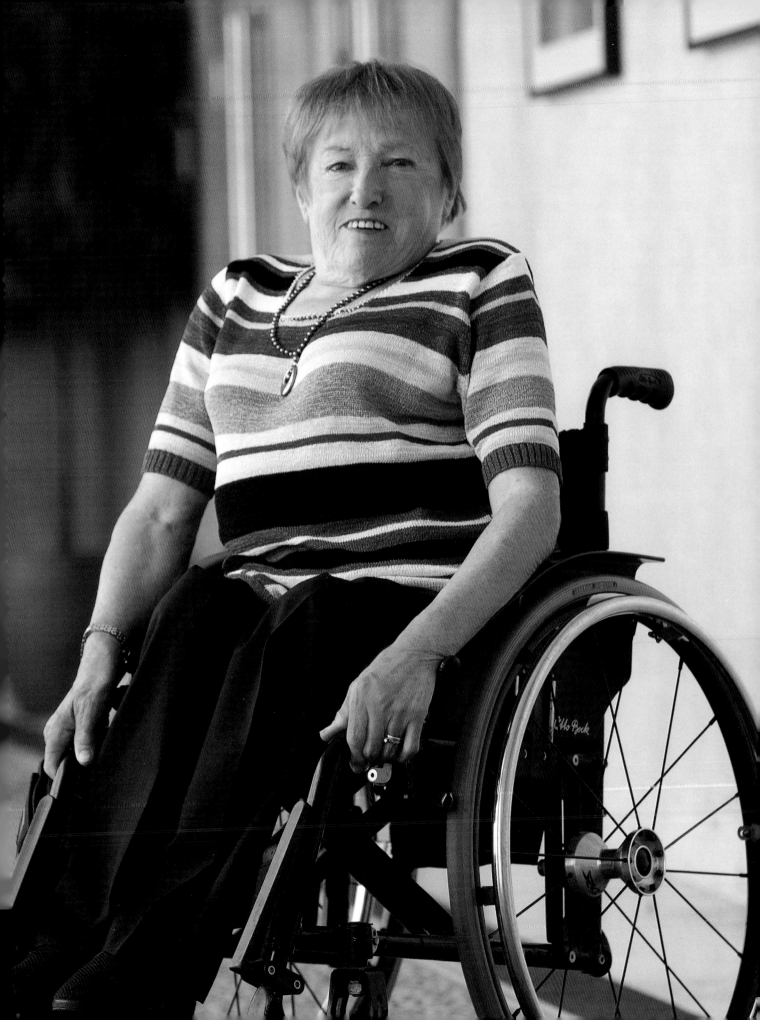

interest in the development of paralympic sports. "We needed to professionalise aspects of sport, including the classification and selection process. Athletes needed to know where they stood and whether they had a realistic chance of competing in the various competitions. There were some fabulous athletes who weren't getting as many opportunities as they should have and I felt that IWA sport needed to be more open and welcoming."

In 1972, Anne, who was by then using a wheelchair most of the time, qualified for the Heidelberg Paralympics with her table tennis partner, Angela Hendra. "It's hard to explain the relief when you finally get the letter to say you've been selected, you've put so much into it at that stage. You are completely gob-smacked with your first Paralympics. I'll never forget the opening ceremony in Heidelberg: stopping in front of the Irish flag, the roar of the crowd, and the adrenaline buzz as you size up the other athletes. You get very patriotic. The experience has never left me and to this day when I watch the opening ceremony on television, I always think of the people who are there for the first time and how they must be feeling. "Sometimes," Anne adds, "I also think of the people who might be there for the last time. One of the things that stands out in my mind was an athlete in Seoul who was in remission from cancer and against the odds won a gold medal. At the closing ceremony, I remember being near her as a big flag went by, saying, 'See you in Barcelona in 1992,' and she turned to me and said, 'You won't see me there.'" Anne won a silver medal at her first Paralympics, and went on to win several more in the years that followed. After Heidelberg, she remembers the exhilaration of her homecoming. "There was great excitement amongst my workmates. They made me bring my medal in and hang it in the window in the shoe factory!"

The inflexible nature of Anne's job made it difficult for her to attend sporting competitions, and in 1975 she decided to take a new position in IWA's Clontarf headquarters. "I started off working as an administrator in the fundraising office, and after a few years, I moved on to the driving school, where I worked with the infamous Micheál and Paddy Saunders. 'Oh, you're too fond of paper work!' Micheál used to say to me."

Anne continued playing table tennis, competing in the Paralympics until 1984, and working voluntarily to develop IWA sports. "I remember at the Toronto Paralympics in 1976, I stayed up till 2am on the night we arrived, checking the entries for our team. These days, nobody would do the administration and compete. But those were the days before funding. It was difficult because sport for people with disabilities wasn't widely acknowledged."

"The profile of IWA sports picked up in 1978 with the establishment of COSPOIR, the National Sports Council," says Anne. "IWA was invited to send a representative to the COSPOIR committee. Lord Dunraven was the first to represent us, followed by Jimmy Byrne in the eighties. Being on this committee opened a few doors, and small bits of funding started coming in." IWA also benefited from fundraising income from the Dublin Milk Run in 1981, the International Year of Disabled Persons, which helped build a sports hall and lay a 100m track in Clontarf. And, in 1986, Anne became IWA's first full-time staff member in the area of sports. "I started off as a sports administrator and later became Director of Sport.

LEFT Anne Ebbs meets President Patrick Hillery at an International Writers Workshop in Mornington, Co Louth, in 1990. IWA members Jimmy Gradwell (centre) and Colm O'Doherty look on

Often, it seemed like I was expected to be all things to all people, until eventually Jimmy Byrne came on board as a full-time sports development officer."

Looking back, Anne says, "We'd never have thought we'd get to the stage we are at today, with a specific Paralympic Council. It's phenomenal. Only in the late nineties, when COSPOIR was replaced by the Sports Council, did serious funding come in. Before then, it was a different world. When we met athletes from other countries, and saw how much better off they were in terms of equipment and coaching, we thought, how do we manage at all? We became more demanding after a while – when you compete at that level you have to be selfish. I remember I suggested they appoint a table tennis coach, and at the Paralympics in Holland in 1980, we had a coach with us for the first time. As an athlete, there is no comparison between being on your own and having a coach with you."

It was through table tennis that Anne met her husband, Tony Ebbs. "Tony was a table tennis player

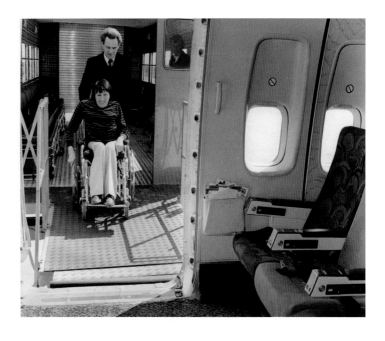

ABOVE Anne uses an ambu-lift to board an Aer Lingus plane at Dublin Airport, as part of an Aer Lingus access audit for passengers with disabilities. The ambu-lift enabled wheelchair users to board safely and with dignity

too, although he'd been unfairly classified like a lot of people with polio. I used to train with him, although he later told me that the first time he'd spoken to me was when I was working in the driving school. Micheál Saunders was a devil for getting members off parking tickets and apparently Tony rang me one day to say he was after getting a ticket and could I help. And I said, 'Well, where were you parked?' and he said, 'On double yellow lines'. 'Well', I told him, unsympathetically, 'What did you expect?' So you're that one, he thought, when he met me some time later, in 1981." Anne and Tony married the following year. "Then, just before Christmas in 1984, he was involved in a fatal car accident on his way to work one morning. The bottom fell out of my world that day. I thought I'd never get over it. I never did, but I learned to cope."

Anne devoted the rest of her career to developing sports, eventually leaving IWA in 1997 to head up the Paralympic Council of Ireland, of which she had been a founder member. She held the position of Secretary General until her retirement in 2008. To mark the occasion of her retirement, she was awarded the International Paralympic Order in recognition of her work, the highest tribute a person connected with the paralympic movement can achieve. The President of the International Paralympic Committee travelled to Drogheda to present the award. "It was a lovely occasion because it gave my family a sense of what I'd been working towards all those years." She also thinks it would have pleased Tony. "He was fanatical about sport and would have been very proud of me." On a final note, Anne adds, "I spent most of my life involved in various aspects of IWA and I've seen the benefits of all aspects of the organisation. If it wasn't for the IWA, a lot of people, me included, wouldn't have had the life they had. And I'm very proud of what I've achieved. It's funny because I've no medals or awards displayed at home – you wouldn't even know I'd picked up a racket. I keep everything in a box at the top of a press. But it doesn't matter because I know what I've got."

Anne Ebbs was Secretary General of the Paralympic Council of Ireland until her retirement in 2008. She lives in Drogheda and continues to be involved in the Paralympic Council as a lifetime honorary board member.

Ronnie Conlon

Driven by a strong work ethic and a determination to live independently

On November 16th, 1966, twenty-year-old Ronnie Conlon was preparing to celebrate the end of his first year of probation in the Gardaí. That morning he had successfully delivered his first court report to a judge. Back at the barracks in Cashel, the sergeant congratulated him and then asked him to go out to chop some wood for the barracks fire. Ronnie and his colleague, Pat, drove off down the back roads to the nearby wood and started work.

While Pat started work with the chainsaw, Ronnie took an axe and went deeper into the woods. As he walked around looking for a suitable tree to fell, the wooden handle of his axe accidentally caught a branch overhead, and the impact rebounded back on him. "It was a one-in-a-million freak accident," says Ronnie. "I couldn't breathe and I fell down. I thought I was having a heart attack. Eventually, I started breathing again and began to struggle back towards Pat. As I walked, I could feel my hands going numb, like they would on a bicycle on a cold winter's day. Pat always did everything by the book, so we gathered up the tools before we left. On our walk to the car, we had to climb over a bull wire fence and in the distance I could see two teams of young lads playing rugby and I remember thinking almost out loud, 'I'm going to die and they don't even know it.' When we got to the car, Pat had to open the passenger door and help me lift my left leg in. As we drove towards Cashel Hospital, Pat steered with one hand and tried to hold me up with the other as I fell left and right with each bend in the road."

Doctors initially suspected Ronnie's fall might have been caused by polio, and later that day he was transferred from Cashel Hospital to Cherry Orchard Hospital in Ballyfermot, County Dublin, which was at that time a fever hospital. "I was there for eight days and eight nights, during which time they sent me out to other hospitals for tests. At night, I could hear the men using the iron lungs in the room beside me. One night there was a power cut, and they all started effing and blinding: 'We'll die! We can't breathe!' I remember thinking, 'At least I'm not in an iron lung'. It's human nature to always be looking for someone worse off than yourself."

Ronnie's doctors eventually came to the conclusion that he had suffered an 'incomplete C5/C6 spinal injury' as the result of a blood clot caused by the impact of the axe handle. Ronnie would need to use a wheelchair and he was moved to the National Rehabilitation Hospital (NRH) to begin the slow process of rehabilitation. Ronnie remembers trying to come to terms with what had happened to him. "My head was racing so fast. I had this constant dream that I was falling off a cliff from a great height. I used to wake up and think, 'Am I paralysed or is this a dream?'." To celebrate Ronnie's 21st birthday, some of his friends and fellow gardaí came up from Cashel and Tuam and brought him out for dinner. "It was very hard. One fellow had to put his arms around my chest in the taxi to hold me up. I didn't feel strong, I didn't feel safe. I didn't feel half the way I wanted to feel."

In the summer of 1970, Ronnie went back to his family home in Tuam for a couple of weeks. "I remember all the kids came running around as the car pulled up and, as they helped me out, one child whispered, 'What's wrong? Are his feet sore?'" In the days that followed, family and friends called in to see him. Ronnie still feels upset as he remembers a visit from his uncle's

ABOVE Ronnie during his first year of probation with the Gardaí

wife. "I was hardly able to sit up on the sofa and when she saw me she started crying. I'll never forget it. She realised more than I did everything I had lost and it made me feel how serious things were. Looking back, I think of what my mother must have been hiding from me as she tried to encourage and support me in those early days. Disability is like a bomb thrown into the middle of a family. No one comes out unscathed. No one comes out whole again."

Ronnie and his parents were hurt by the way the Garda authorities handled his accident. "It grates to this day that none of the senior gardaí came to see me in hospital. Over time, it became clear that I was not going to be offered any feasible way in which I could complete my probation.

"Disability is like a bomb thrown into the middle of a family. No one comes out unscathed"

No one had the courage or gumption to say that to me directly, but they must have communicated it to the hospital authorities because eventually the social worker let me know I had to start looking into other options. In January 1968, a garda sergeant was finally sent down to the hospital to hand me my certificate of service, formally discharging me."

With his career in the Gardaí at an end, staff at the NRH encouraged Ronnie to begin a BA in English, History and Philosophy at UCD that autumn. "College was good for me. I began to socialise again and meet new people. But I knew I was on a loser academically. It was too early in my recovery. I was living in a ward with a lot of sick men and I wasn't organised enough to manage the work. I couldn't write myself, so an elderly lady with a Remington typewriter would transcribe my work. Eventually, after failing my exams, the NRH let me know that it was time to go back home for good."

Back in Tuam, Ronnie surprised everyone by getting a job with a database management and direct mail firm. "My mother would help me up at six in the morning and my father would bring me in and out, stopping for a pint on the way home." The job lasted until 1974 when the first oil crisis led to the closure of the company. "By that stage, I had proven to myself and to others that I could work and earn a living." Ronnie quickly went on to get another job in a company called Digital, based in Galway City. "Digital was known as a progressive employer and I was determined to succeed. I remember saying in the interview: 'If I'm not up to the job, I promise you won't be worrying about how to get rid of me; I'll be the first to go.'"

But Ronnie was still relying on others for transport to and from work. "My father left me in Tuam town every morning and I'd wait for a lift to Galway, sometimes in harsh weather. The Galway branch of IWA would give me a lift a couple of days a week and the other days I had to organise local drivers. I was starting to miss days and I knew if I wanted to keep working, I had to get my own car." Ronnie's friends saw his predicament and started fundraising: "The lads in Digital organised a dance and some young fellows in Tuam organised a sponsored swim. I also got tremendous support from the ordinary Gardaí in Tuam." In the summer of 1975, Ronnie bought his DAF 66 car and, after a few lessons with Micheál Saunders, started driving to work. "I believe that if I hadn't got assistance at that particular time, it could have been curtains for me in terms of working."

Ronnie also became involved in IWA. "It started through social events and holidays, and I went on to join the IWA National Council. We had our meetings at Adare Manor, and there was a great mix of characters involved, such as Liam Maguire, who I always thought of as the real boss of IWA, and Lord Dunraven, whose speeches delivered an incredible impact. Ronnie's links with IWA also opened his eyes to the emerging disability rights movement abroad. In 1976, he attended a housing conference in Denmark. "It was my first trip to a Scandinavian country and it blew my mind entirely. We went to people's houses and saw how they were living. One lady who had been in a nursing home for years had convinced the authorities that she could live independently and was training as a farm manager. I liked the Danish people and I came away with a realisation of what could be done if you had the right attitude."

Ronnie began to reflect on his own living situation. "All this time I'd been living in the family home. I remember a friend from UCD came down to visit me and she brought me a book of Robert Frost's poetry. In it, she had written: 'You've got to get out of this place!' And, do you know what? It was the truth!"

Ronnie says he became aware of a big difference in the ways in which Catholic and non-Catholic countries supported their citizens with disabilities. Scandinavian countries were proactive about employment and independence. "You can talk all you like about disability, but if a man has a job, he has a much better chance of independence, a normal life, and some respect from others," says Ronnie. Whereas Catholic countries like Ireland expected the mother to become a carer. "I tried to imagine what it was like for my mother. When I came home from hospital, she'd had to give up a good job as a supervisor in Erin foods. In the morning, everything I needed would be set out ready for me. 'Are you okay? Do you have everything you need?' she would ask every few minutes. Only when I went out the door could she start to live her own life."

ABOVE Ronnie as a young boy pictured beside a turf stack. Ronnie remembers many days spent 'footing the turf' and says that the only good thing about being paralysed was that he never had to foot the turf again

Ronnie applied for social housing and was allocated a house in Galway. "That was the easy part. But I couldn't move out without a commitment from the Health Board to provide me with at least an hour and a half's help every morning. I raised the problem at an IWA conference in Adare in 1978. I remember one of the IWA occupational therapists stood up and said, 'You go back to the Health Board and tell them if they don't sort you out, I'll personally gather forty people in wheelchairs to protest outside their offices.' It felt brilliant to have that support and on the Monday afterwards I rang the Health Board and threatened them with our protest. Within a week, my assistance had been approved."

Ronnie moved out in 1978 and has lived independently ever since, eventually buying his home from the local authority. He says he has lived a good life, although he admits to occasional regrets at not having married. "I had a few near misses, but for one reason or another it didn't happen and, to tell the honest truth, I do regret that. I was always conscious that I didn't want to make someone an addendum to me, always having to care for me and put me first. And I suppose over the years I haven't always been able to give enough, either because I haven't felt up to it or because it takes so much energy just to take care of myself. Life isn't perfect and I have learnt that you have to play the hand you're dealt."

Ronnie went back to college in NUI Galway in 1992, completing a BA in Education and English, before moving on to a HDip in 1994. He currently works for IWA's Advocacy Service.

Michael Cunningham, winner of the wheelchair category in the Dublin City Marathon in 1981, approaches the finish line

Irish Wheelchair Association in the
1980s

ABOVE **Ronnie Conlon, Galway, gives his opinions on the way forward for the Association at a seminar in Adare Manor, 1980** LEFT **Taoiseach Charles Haughey poised to cut the tape to start the Milk Run in Dublin's Phoenix Park, 1981** BELOW **Member Nora Alford demonstrating an accessible kitchen**

1980 — **1981** — **1982**

FEBRUARY 1980
IWA Adare Seminar
By 1980, IWA's staff included driving instructors, social workers, occupational therapists, wheelchair mechanics, community workers, fundraisers and administrators. IWA had fifty-two branches across Ireland and membership had risen to 2,850. In February 1980, over a hundred members, staff and branch representatives gathered in Adare Manor, home of IWA President, Lord Dunraven, for a seminar to discuss the future of the Association. One new development which emerged as a result of the seminar was the introduction of committees, which would be set up on a regional basis, to begin to plan and co-ordinate projects for the International Year of Disabled Persons in 1981.

JULY 1980
Paralympic Games in Arnham, Holland
In July 1980, the Paralympics were held in Arnhem, Holland. Although Moscow was the venue for the Olympic Games, the city was unable to host the Paralympics due to the lack of accessible facilities. A team of twenty-three Irish athletes travelled to the games along with staff, including team manager Jimmy Byrne. Gold medallists included: Rosaleen Gallagher,

who competed in the pentathlon; Julie Toomey, who competed in table tennis; and Bill Ensor and Paul Smyth, who competed in men's bowls. Silver and bronze medals were also won in the club-throw, discus and shot-putt events.

1981
International Year of Disabled Persons
1981 was proclaimed the International Year of Disabled Persons (IYDP) by the United Nations. As part of the occasion, the UN called for a plan of action which focused on equalisation of opportunities, rehabilitation and prevention of disabilities. The IYDP helped raise public awareness regarding the right of people with

disabilities to take part fully in all aspects of society and to enjoy living conditions equal to those of other citizens. The year was launched on New Year's Eve by the Lord Mayor of Dublin, Fergus O'Brien, TD, at the Mansion House, Dublin. Liam Maguire was nominated as Chairman of the Committee of IYDP and, during the year, IWA focused on raising awareness through media opportunities, including the appearance of Lord Dunraven, Liam Maguire and Brian Malone on *The Late Late Show*.

FEBRUARY 1981
IWA housing policy launched
On February 11th, 1981, IWA launched its *Housing Policy for Physically Disabled People* in the Gresham Hotel, Dublin. This document recommended that five percent of local authority housing be made suitable for people in wheelchairs and that a "generous and sensitively administered grant scheme" be provided for the adaptation of private housing.

MARCH 1981
IWA selected as 'Milk Run' charity
In light of the International Year of Disabled Persons, IWA was selected as the charity of choice for the National Dairy Council's annual

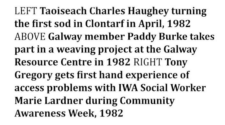

LEFT **Taoiseach Charles Haughey turning the first sod in Clontarf in April, 1982** ABOVE **Galway member Paddy Burke takes part in a weaving project at the Galway Resource Centre in 1982** RIGHT **Tony Gregory gets first hand experience of access problems with IWA Social Worker Marie Lardner during Community Awareness Week, 1982**

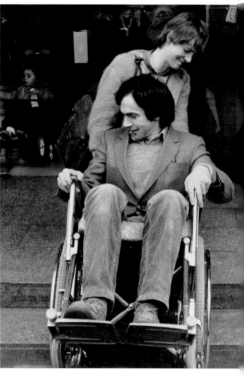

1983   **1984**

'Milk Run' in 1981. The main run was held on March 22nd in the Phoenix Park, Dublin, with approximately two hundred smaller runs being organised throughout the country. Hundreds of IWA members along with friends, family and Gardaí participated alongside the general public. The money raised would go towards the building of the new sports hall and day care centre in Clontarf.

OCTOBER 1981
Dublin City Marathon
The first Dublin City Marathon in 1980 was not open to wheelchair athletes, however this changed in 1981 when, after meetings between the organisers and IWA representatives, the Dublin City Marathon became one of the first marathons in Europe to introduce a wheelchair category. Athlete Michael Cunningham was first to complete the 26.2 miles and win the wheelchair category.

APRIL 1982
Taoiseach lays foundation stone in Clontarf
The money raised during the 1981 Milk Run helped fund the construction of a sports hall on the grounds of the Association's headquarters in Clontarf. Taoiseach Charles

Haughey laid the foundation stone for the building in April 1982. The approximate cost of the project was £650,000.

JUNE 1982
IWA policy on access and mobility
In June 1982, IWA published a policy document titled, *Accessibility and Mobility for Physically Disabled Persons*. Speaking at the launch, Liam Maguire criticised CIÉ for failing to provide accessible public transport. He said CIE had had an ideal opportunity to incorporate facilities for people with disabilities in its new Bombardier buses but had refused to do so. Liam Maguire also referred to the draft Building Regulations, which contained a section making it illegal to build inaccessible public buildings. Despite promises by successive Governments, the Regulations had been in draft form since 1976 and had not been enacted. In accepting the first copy of the document, Minister for the Environment, Ray Burke, TD, promised to keep the matter high on his priority list.

JUNE 1982
Promoting awareness amongst public reps
IWA's social services department and volunteers throughout the country were

consistently promoting awareness of disability amongst their local public representatives. In the summer of 1982, IWA social worker Marie Lardner accompanied newly elected Independent TD Tony Gregory as he made his way around the city in a wheelchair during Community Awareness Week. A similar exercise was undertaken in 1985 when Lord Mayor of Dublin, Michael O'Halloran, became a wheelchair user for a day and attempted to carry out tasks such as opening a bank account, visiting the Pro-Cathedral, making a phone call from a phone box, and having lunch in a café.

JANUARY 1983
Home Care Attendant scheme begins
An IWA Home Care Attendant pilot scheme based in North Dublin received funding for a six-month trial beginning in January, 1983. The plan was to provide the care that people with disabilities needed, particularly in times of crisis when relatives were not available or were unable to cope. By providing this support in people's homes, the scheme aimed to enable people to live as independently as possible within the community. By May, twenty-seven families were availing of the service and demand for the service had begun to increase

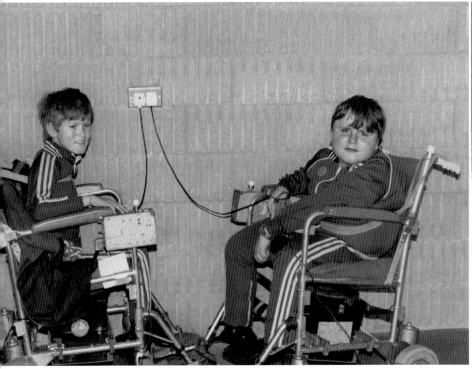

ABOVE **Young athletes racing on the newly laid track in IWA Clontarf** LEFT **Two young members charging their power wheelchairs in preparation for a race**

1985　　　　　　　　1986　　　　　　　　1987

dramatically. The Home Care Attendant scheme was operating nationally by the mid-1980s. The scheme is considered a fundamental step towards the Assisted Living Services which operate today.

SEPTEMBER 1983
Liam Maguire dies
On September 16th, 1983, Liam Maguire, lobbyist, advocate and one of the most influential players in the disability movement, died at the age of forty.

APRIL 1984
Government green paper on disability
In April 1984, the Government published its long awaited green paper on disability, *Towards a Full Life*. The paper covered the topics of employment, training, income maintenance, community services, access, transport and residential care for people with disabilities. The National Rehabilitation Board was to have responsibility for promoting goals of full participation and equality, and for stimulating the development of policies and services. IWA was disheartened by the paper, and IWA researcher Pauline Faughnan commented, "In general terms, the green paper

is a very disappointing document, both in its philosophy and in terms of practical proposals."

JULY 1984
The Paralympic Games – New York and Stoke Mandeville
Bad planning resulted in the 1984 Paralympics, which had been awarded to New York, being split between two venues. The two venues were New York, USA, which held competitions for the ambulant and amputee athletes and Stoke Mandeville, UK, which held competitions for the wheelchair athletes. This was a source of disappointment to many of the wheelchair athletes who had been looking forward to competing in the USA. At the games, young Irish athlete Ronan Tynan from Kilkenny stole the limelight, winning three gold medals and one bronze, and setting world records in discus, shot-putt and long jump. He was also awarded 'Best overall athlete' of the games.

JANUARY 1985
Day care centre opens in Clontarf
IWA's purpose-built day care facility in Clontarf, built at a total cost of £624,000, opened its doors in January 1985. The first programme to start was a pre-vocational training programme.

By March, a day care programme, and recreational and independent living training programmes had been introduced. The centre catered for up to eighty people each day.

APRIL 1986
Promoting independent living
The Association acquired a semi-detached house at the entrance to its headquarters in Clontarf in 1983 and, in 1985, plans were drawn up to develop the house and adjoining land into six independent housing units which could be used to provide training in independent living as well as short-term leases for members on housing lists. At the end of the tenancy, it was hoped that members would move on to suitable housing having gained confidence and skills.

APRIL 1986
Establishment of four IWA regions
At the Association's AGM in the West County Hotel, Ennis, on April 19th - 20th, significant constitutional changes were introduced which involved the development of four IWA regions, around which budgets, staffing and plans would be based. These were to be South East, West/North West, Midland/North East and South/Mid West.

RIGHT **IWA Chairman Colm O'Doherty pictured in Ballyfermot Library, which had received recognition for its high level of accessibility** ABOVE **Donncha O'Dúlaing in costume at the Brian Ború march from Clare to Clontarf in April 1988** BELOW **Development of the sports hall, Clontarf, gets under way**

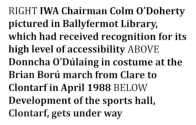

1988   1989

MARCH 1987
Beginning of creative writing programme
In 1987 the Association held creative writing workshops in Kilkenny, Dublin and Tralee, and through many local branches. In spring 1989 a publication titled *From Think to Ink*, which consisted of the writings by participants of a writers' workshop held in the Midlands/North East region, was launched by Taoiseach Garret Fitzgerald. All five hundred copies were sold.

APRIL 1988
Brian Ború fundraising march
On April 3rd - 16th, 1988, IWA, in partnership with Inagh Community Association and Clontarf GAA Club, held the Brian Ború fundraising march from Clare to Clontarf, with Donncha O'Dúlaing as march leader. The historically themed event featured period costume and was inspired by the Dublin Millennium Celebrations.

OCTOBER 1988
Seoul Paralympics
The 1988 Paralympic Games are remembered by many as the games which set the Paralympics on an equal footing to the Olympics. They were held two weeks after the Olympic Games, using the same competition and accommodation venues,

and the same support services. More importantly, the Paralympic athletes were treated with the same high esteem as their Olympic counterparts. This established a standard by which all future Paralympics would be judged. It also lay the foundations of partnership between the International Paralympic Committee and the International Olympic Committee, which would eventually lead to an agreement being signed in 2000 under which all cities bidding to host the Olympic Games would also have to host the Paralympic Games. The Irish team returned with thirteen gold medals, ten silvers and fourteen bronzes, receiving a hero's welcome at

Dublin Airport. Aer Rianta opened an area on the roof of the airport to accommodate the many fans who turned out to welcome the team.

MAY 1989
Official opening of Clontarf
On May 19th, 1989, the official opening by An Taoiseach, Charles Haughey, of the day care centre, the wheelchair sales and repair workshop, independent living units and sports hall in Clontarf took place. Although some facilities had been in operation for several years, the opening marked the end of a major period of development.

Martin Naughton

A pioneer of the independent living movement

Martin Naughton has been at the centre of the move away from institutional living that has characterised the past few decades. He has fought hard to ensure that all people, regardless of their level of disability, are given the option of living independently. Interestingly, Martin believes that the political instincts which have made him such an effective advocate were honed by his own institutional upbringing in St Mary's Hospital in Baldoyle. "Those of us who grew up in institutions learnt how to read situations very quickly at an early age. You learn how to rebel in a clever way. Timing is a big part of everything. Sometimes you get so used to seeing round corners, that the difficulty you have later in life is remembering that others don't see the same thing."

Martin and his younger sister, Barbara, came to Baldoyle in 1963 when he was nine years of age. "I was born in Spiddal, Galway, so my first language was Irish. Moving to Baldoyle was like moving to a foreign country. Everybody spoke a different language and there was very little green around." Martin was one of eight children, three of whom were diagnosed with spinal muscular atrophy. "In layman's language, if you think of muscles as light bulbs and nerves as wiring, all my bulbs are in great shape, but there is very little power supply getting to them. And, as it is a progressive disability, the power supply becomes less every year. I was four years old when it became noticeable and by eight years of age I was a wheelchair user. So basically my life has been as a wheelchair user."

"The sister who ran Baldoyle was nicknamed the 'White Tornado'," says Martin. "The White Tornado could give Nurse Ratched (from the film *One Flew over the Cuckoo's Nest*) a run for her money most of the time but every now and then she showed a little heart. The secret was to see if you could challenge something and live to see another day. I was lucky because I found ways of making myself useful. From around 1966 onwards, I went out on all the flag days and collections, and I would be given the job of looking for collection licences or counting money. I had an opportunity to get to know the White Tornado in a different way, and occasionally she'd confide in me. She was a very interesting person, a late vocation, who had been in hotel management or something like that before she joined the convent. I got myself into that situation through boredom perhaps, but it came naturally to me to find ways of working the system. The only stumbling block was learning English at the beginning." Martin adds: "I don't want to pretend that it was a lovely, happy place. It was a tough place. Everybody lived in fear. Not just the children, the staff too. I'm not trying to justify it or soften it, but it was of its time in many ways. It was particularly hard for children who had no family. There was a good understanding amongst staff and patients of who had nobody, who had people hardly worth talking about, and who had people who might be somebody. Despite that, there wasn't much teasing amongst the children. The one thing we had in common was that we were all at the bottom of the heap, no matter what our father's name was."

In the late 1960s, Martin set up Baldoyle Hospital Sports Club (BHSC) and began organising sporting competitions. "We had table tennis competitions and football matches. Crowds of local children would gather around the railings, dying to join in. I got to grips with the rules and became the main organiser. There were very few competitions for young people so we entered our athletes into adult competitions. We had people with amazing skill, like Kathleen Reynolds and Michael Cunningham – or the 'blond dynamite' as he was known. I never competed, but I loved seeing our people winning."

Martin was a natural networker, getting to know many influential people, such as Billy McNeill, Captain of Glasgow Celtic Football Club. "Billy and myself became good friends. He'd have me over to Celtic as his guest. He even bought me my first motorised wheelchair in the late sixties. I also got to know Frank Stapleton, a great Arsenal and Manchester United player and one of Ireland's greatest centre forwards, who used to visit Baldoyle. Any time Frank was man of the match, which was pretty often at the time, a thousand pounds went straight into the BHSC bank account. In my experience, celebrities are often willing to help – they just need to be asked, and I never minded asking."

Martin's impact on Baldoyle was so significant that when he was sixteen he received special permission to stay on for two extra years, rather than be transferred to a Cheshire Home. "I was attending a local secondary school and studying for my Leaving, and I knew I was valuable to them in terms of fundraising and organisation. Also, they had opened a swimming pool which they couldn't afford to run, and I convinced them I could make it pay." By 1972, Martin had been given a full-time job as Baldoyle's first recreation manager. "I have to credit the people who took the chance on me. It was a plum job. I was responsible for the kids outside of school, physiotherapy and care time. So I set about undoing the routine that had defined Baldoyle for decades. I would say to the children, 'I think we should have tea in a different place today. Where would you like to have tea?'" Martin adds that his aims were not entirely altruistic. "I was very much into sport, recreation and community development, but I didn't have any great master plan. Of course, part of it was that I was eighteen years of age and I wanted to get paid. I loved life. I was determined to live life on my own terms, and I needed beer money!"

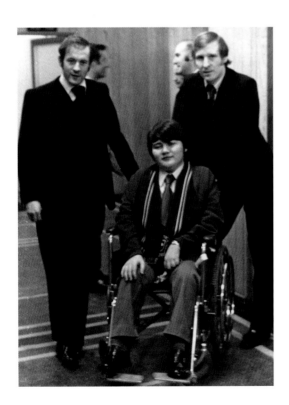

ABOVE Glasgow Celtic Manager Billy McNeill (right), who invited Martin to the Celtic grounds as a special guest

In 1973, Martin went to Germany to complete a course in sports and recreation for people with disabilities. "It was wonderful. The course was connected with Sir Ludwig Guttmann [founder of the Paralympics], and on my way back to Ireland, I spent a few weeks with him in Stoke Mandeville in the UK. Sir Ludwig was the inspiration for a different approach. He was the first person to name the fact that disability was going to be with us for a long time, and to talk about living with a disability. The world was changing and I'd seen that with my own eyes in Baldoyle. Polio was nearly eradicated but there were new kinds of disabilities, things like spina bifida, muscular dystrophy and paralysis. Before then, people hadn't survived these conditions but that was changing, and Sir Ludwig saw sport as a way of improving health and increasing community participation."

For a brief spell in 1974, Martin moved from Baldoyle to the newly opened Cheshire Home in the Phoenix Park. "I was the first resident there. It was a great facility but it was cut off from the community. I described it to Leonard Cheshire himself, who in fairness was always open to suggestions, as a 'Grade A hotel in the middle of the Sahara Desert'. I was there for three months, getting a taxi to work in Baldoyle every day, before I decided to move back into Baldoyle."

Martin says that during the 1970s and 1980s the culture at Baldoyle began to change. "Baldoyle's greatest asset was that every part of it reached onto a public road; it was not hidden down a long avenue. Most of the staff were locals, so it seemed natural to open the place up to the community and make it the centre of the parish. We became involved with Girl Guide and Scout groups, and in the re-formation of Baldoyle Football Club. There began to be young people in the community who were authorities on disability, and who had best friends with disabilities. And IWA was only a stone's throw away in Clontarf, so our big athletes were moving on to train and compete there. Jimmy Byrne got involved as a volunteer, and he became one of the guys who in his own way dared us to dream even bigger dreams. The White Tornado retired and Baldoyle started to feel less like a hospital and more like a residential centre. It was changing, bit by bit, and with it came new expectations for the young people who had grown up there."

When the International Year of Disabled Persons arrived in 1981, Martin wanted to do something special. "I lined up some business people and we arranged for a load of kids with disabilities, who had never had a holiday, to go to the Algarve. While planning the trip, I got to know business people from Baldoyle and Malahide and got on well with them. One fellow kept saying, 'When this is done, we'll have to do some real work together and make some money!' It planted a seed in my mind and at the end of 1981, I said to him, 'Okay, let's get on with it!' By that time, life was getting pretty good for people with disabilities who could live independently without a great deal of support. I felt it was time to leave the world of disability behind, so I threw in the towel at Baldoyle. I moved out into a private, rented house, and set up my own business doing crash repairs. When it came to cars, all I knew was that they came in different colours, but I hired decent people and I learned as I went. I built the business up and sold it on in 1987, by which stage I was working as a consultant to a number of businesses.

"In order to live independently, I relied on assistance from a number of private PAs. A lot of it was informal. One of the guys who helped me was the painter who did the colour matching on the crash repairs. And some local families would help out. I was a hand-me-down. There are very few fellows of thirty-five plus in Baldoyle who didn't put me to bed or look after me for a couple of nights a week for a year or two. None of that would be allowed to happen today. We've become so over protective and have reined everyone in with health and safety legislation."

"I began to think about all the people back home, many of whom I had semi-reared in some sense, who were living in institutions"

In the late 1980s, Martin began to travel to the States regularly. "I had a nice little business bringing students on J1 visas to the US. In January and February, I'd visit the colleges and round up five hundred students. Then I'd line up accommodation and jobs for them in New York and Boston. I'd always wanted to travel and I was spending six months of the year over there. My office and accommodation was in Beacon Street, in the heart of Boston, and I felt like I had a new energy when I was there. It was all going so well that I was thinking of finding my way to the States permanently." While in Boston, Martin came into contact with the Boston Center for Independent Living. "If I wanted accessible tickets for a game at Fenway Park, I had to go down to the Center and after a while I got to know them. They said, 'On Friday evening we shut up shop early and talk. Why don't you come around and join us?' So I ended up meeting people who were just like me, who were running independent living centres for other people with disabilities. I spent time with them, exploring the whole notion of independent living. And I began to think about all the people back home, many of whom I had semi-reared in some sense when I was in Baldoyle, who were living in institutions. The temptation to do something became too great and I felt the pull back home."

Martin says that from about 1988 he "started transferring the ideas from the Center for Independent Living in Boston to a group of people here. I had become a board member of IWA and started telling people about my vision. There were some very good people on the board at the time, including some older people like Jim Molloy, former City Manager, and others such as Brian Malone, Colm O'Doherty, Jim Dukes (Alan Duke's father) and founder member Jack Kerrigan."

By 1990 an informal group had been set up with the aim of furthering the cause of independent living. "We met regularly in the IWA's information centre, where we sat around a big long table and discussed areas in which we could target change. There were ten or twelve of us in the group, all IWA people, including Michael McCabe, Dermot Walsh, Peter Moore, Declan O'Keeffe, Hubert McCormack, the late Denis O'Brien, the late Ursula Hegarty and Dolores Murphy. We used to name ourselves something different every week, depending on the area we were focusing on. The big issues, known as the pillars of independent living, were housing, mobility, PAs and technology.

"The focus of the group was on independent living for people for whom it wasn't straightforward to live independently, people who required significant supports," says Martin. Eventually the decision was taken to set up a separate organisation, which could focus completely on establishing supports for independent living, and specifically on targeting funding for personal assistance services. "I stepped down from the board of IWA to channel all my energy into the task at hand. I knew what we wanted was going to require a father and mother of a battle, and I think people appreciated that. It wasn't a negative breakaway, it was just a way of giving priority to this project. We needed to be in a position to take charge and to take risks."

This breakaway group formally became the Center [sic] for Independent Living (CIL) in March 1992, although Martin says the group was effectively running from the late 1980s. "Our priority was to secure funding in a hugely competitive environment. The launch of the National Lottery in 1987 had been seen as a big threat to fundraising, and donor fatigue was the phrase being bandied about at the time." The CIL put together an application for European money under the Horizon scheme and was granted half a million pounds to train twenty-five PAs for fifteen significantly disabled people to live independently in their own community. "From the start our plan was carefully thought out. When we got the Horizon money, we went straight to the Department of Social Welfare and said, 'We can create jobs', and they gave us additional core funding of £50,000 a year. Then we went to FÁS, and said, 'We want these jobs to be for good,' and came away with an agreement that every PA would be taken on under the job training scheme, providing us with a grant of seventy percent of their salary. All of a sudden our half a million was growing, and we knew we could do something significant.

"We hired PAs and ran training programmes in IWA Clontarf and the Carmichael Centre," says Martin. "The PAs were allocated to a mix of people, most of whom took the opportunity to move out of institutional homes into rented accommodation. Our big thing was that we wanted people with disabilities to ask themselves, 'Is this accommodation right for you? Are you in charge of your own life? Are you doing what you want to do?' That was the CIL ethos. We saw it as an opportunity to push boundaries and perceptions of disability, and we showed up everywhere we could with our PAs to make sure people knew what we were doing." The CIL rapidly received further European funding, which they used to develop the service. "We set up a new programme called 'Operation Get-Out'. It was aimed at people living in Cheshire homes, who had been in a home for the whole of their lives. We wanted to give these people an opportunity to be free at last. We put up notices in the Cheshire homes and targeted about ten individuals, many of whom I knew from my early days in Baldoyle. People were afraid to leave in case they would lose their place and end up somewhere worse, but the management in Cheshire was very supportive and agreed to guarantee their places for one year. They understood that having security would lift a weight off people's shoulders. Remember, nobody had done this before and it's not easy being the first to jump."

One of the people who signed up for Operation Get-Out was IWA member Mairéad Manton, who has cerebral palsy. "Mairéad was in her mid-thirties and had lived in institutions her whole life. In many ways hers was a horrendous story, but I don't know how to describe the courage, determination and persistence that Mairéad showed. There are not enough words in the English language to describe it, and any day, I'd gladly take my hat off to her. She was brave enough to step out into a world that was utterly and completely unknown. But she did it all at her own pace and survived. Not every participant in Operation Get-Out took to independent living," adds Martin. "A couple of people went back to the institutional homes, having decided that independent living wasn't for them. I remember being disappointed at first, but then I insisted that we celebrate because they had made their choice. They'd been given the option of staying or going – and nobody else before them had had that."

Having proved the viability of the PA model, CIL set about devising a strategy to attract long-term funding. "Getting EU money was no problem, but we always knew the real challenge was going to be home-grown money. How could we sustain the service beyond the three-year period of Horizon funding?" Martin and his CIL colleagues knew there would be many organisations competing for domestic funding at the end of the Horizon programme so they took the strategic decision to begin campaigning very early. "We deliberately brought the crisis forward by six months so we could have the whole stage to ourselves. We built up a strong media profile and staged a night-long protest outside the Dáil on the last session before the summer break in June 1994. Eventually, at about 4 a.m., Brendan Howlin, who was Minister for Health, issued a statement to say that we would be funded for a further three to six months while they conducted a full evaluation.

The evaluation took nearly a year to complete, complicated by a change in Government and the appointment of a new Minister for Health, Michael Noonan. "It was the most difficult year of my life. I remember one evening I met Minister Noonan in the Coffee Dock in Jury's Hotel and I

ABOVE Martin protesting outside the Dáil in June 1994 as part of CIL's campaign for funding for personal assistant services

caught up with him in the toilets. 'I know what you are going to ask me,' he said as he walked towards the door, 'and I want to tell you that you have nothing to worry about. It's put to bed.' That night was the first night I'd slept well in years."

In June 1995, the evaluation report was published, strongly supporting the long-term viability of the PA concept, and Government funding was approved. "We had secured Irish money that they could never take away again," says Martin. Having won this landmark battle, Martin says CIL had done its job. "We had never intended to become a service provider and we wanted to move on to other key issues like transport, so the Department of Health asked IWA to take over the operation of the PA service, an arrangement which has continued until today." Martin believes the success of this campaign, and of many of his earlier projects, was partly down to timing. "If I was starting over tomorrow, even with all the knowledge of the past fifty years, I couldn't do it all again. I got a lot of breaks. Disability used to open a lot of doors. I never had to queue. I had the ear of important people. Even celebrities were nervous around people with disabilities, and I'd spend time putting them at ease. That has all changed. There is a part of me that would love to go back to the way things were, but of course intellectually I know it's a good thing that I don't get special treatment!"

Martin continues to advocate for the principles of independent living, conscious of the risks of complacency. "For example, one thing we have to be careful of now is that we don't institutionalise people's own homes by over-regulating the way in which PA services are delivered. People should have as much flexibility as possible about the way they live their lives." He adds: "We have achieved a great deal over the past fifty years, and the credit for what has been achieved so far belongs to no organisation, it belongs to people with disabilities themselves."

Martin currently works for the Disability Federation of Ireland (DFI) and is a board member and consultant for the European Network on Independent Living (ENIL).

Paddy Saunders and Micheál Saunders

Making it as easy as possible for members to start driving

The Saunders brothers, Paddy and Micheál, taught thousands of members to drive in their forty years as driving instructors with IWA. "I remember in the early days," says Micheál, "the branches would complain: 'We've never seen so and so since you taught them how to drive'. And for a while they were up in arms about it. But eventually they understood. The whole idea was that members could be independent, go to dances with their friends or do whatever the hell they wanted to do. They didn't have to rely on IWA or any other outfit."

Paddy, who has limited mobility in his right arm and hand, became involved as a member and volunteer before being taken on as a driver. "In the early sixties, I used to work down in the Pearse Street office," says Paddy. "Mrs Dowling was there and she used to wind me up something fierce! She got wise that I knew how to get into certain places and she used to play on that. We'd do flag days and collections in the cattle markets. Mrs Dowling had the gift of the gab, so I'd just do the driving and let her and the members off to do their thing." By the mid-1960s, Paddy had recruited his brother Micheál as a volunteer driver. Micheál remembers collecting members from the Royal Hospital, Donnybrook, and from Cheshire Homes around Dublin. "Members used to look forward to going out on the flag days. If you were sitting there twiddling your fingers every day, you'd be glad to get out, to wherever it was."

In the early days, Paddy and Micheál used ordinary Minis to collect members, squashing in as many people as possible and strapping the wheelchairs to the back of the cars. The acquisition of IWA's first bus in 1967 made journeys more comfortable,

LEFT Paddy Saunders with the IWA Volkswagen mini-bus in the late 1960s

although getting members on and off was hard work. "There was no such thing as bus adaptations in those days," says Micheál. "You had to lift members in, even if they were twenty stone, or they didn't come. We didn't get buses with lifts until 1970 when the CRC gave us some of their old buses."

By the late 1960s, Paddy and Micheál were regularly giving informal driving lessons to members. Micheál remembers the awkwardness of teaching in three-wheeled cars. "The social welfare in England gave every disabled person one of those cars, and some of our members used to bring them in second-hand. They were awful looking and highly dangerous, as well as anti-social because there was no space for anyone to travel

ABOVE IWA staff member Peter Stokes (left), with a member, and Paddy Saunders on an IWA holiday in Monaghan in the 1970s. Many members availed of lessons from the IWA driving school while on holiday

with you. While we were instructing, we had to crouch in the back behind the driver. The driving testers treated them as motorbikes and wouldn't even get into them."

In 1972, IWA opened a driving school and Micheál became its first employee. "I remember the first day I came in, there was this 1100 Austin – a total banger – and I thought, how are we going to teach anyone in this?" Micheál set about professionalising the service. "We needed proper cars and insurance. In those days nobody knew anything about driving with a disability. There were no companies supplying hand controls and the insurance companies thought we should be getting disabled people off the roads, not onto them. If you got a quote it would be doubled or tripled at the mention of disability."

Micheál was given a list of members who wanted to learn to drive by one of IWA's social workers, Mary King. "They were all over the place. I remember one day I went to a house in Finglas and this old lady answered the door. 'I'm here to give you a driving lesson,' I said. 'Oh, I don't want to drive,' she replied, 'but I need to go down to the chemist to get stockings, if you wouldn't mind driving me?' The old lady was lonesome and she thought that signing up for driving lessons would be a great way of getting out!

"I began to think there had to be a better system than going out to people's houses. I was sitting jammed in traffic all day, doing nothing most of the time. I decided that if members wanted to drive, they needed to put a bit of effort in and come to us in Clontarf. If they did that, I didn't mind if it took us two years to teach them. There was no reason to give up just because they were slow. If we thought they could get there in the end, we'd stick with it."

Within a year of the opening, Paddy had joined Micheál as a full-time driving instructor, and the Association had invested in four new Minis with hand controls. The driving school also started organising adaptations for members' cars. "There was no one doing hand controls in Ireland so we got a book on hand controls from a place in Sydenham in south London. We used to go over, buy them, bring them back, and then get McMeel's Engineering in South Gloucester Street to fit them. The whole idea was to make it as simple and easy as possible for a disabled person to drive. The way to do that was an automatic car with push/pull hand controls and a knob on the steering wheel."

The driving school expanded steadily throughout the 1970s. Esther Delaney and Nora Alford, Micheál's first two students, began working on the switch, and permanent instructors were taken on in Cork in 1973 and Galway in 1979. "Before then, lessons had been given by volunteers and lads from the Guards. They did a great job but things had to

> ## *"All that counted at the end of the day was the member and if you could do anything at all for them, you'd do it"*

ABOVE Micheál Saunders assists as athlete Michael Cunningham disembarks the IWA bus at Stoke Mandeville

move on because it was such an important service."

Micheál believes driving enabled members to work. "If you couldn't drive, you'd go into an interview and the employer would say, 'Where do you live? Do I have to pick you up and bring you in?' He'd be thinking how much it would cost to do all that, not to mention adapt the building. A lot of businesses were struggling to exist and you had to see it from their side. So it was a great thing when a member went for an interview and was able to respond, 'Oh, I can drive and get myself here. No problem!'

"I used to advise members not to go along to interviews with all this righteous stuff," adds Micheál. "I'd say, don't start giving out about the toilets not being right or the ramp. Just do your best. You want a job and your man's willing to pay you. So take it, work well, and eventually when you've got on a bit and he's doing some alterations, say, 'Now, don't forget me when you do that work.' In my mind, the worst thing was to put a picket on a workplace. That was the way Paddy and I looked at it anyway."

While driving could improve employment prospects, most members started out with no income and needed support to purchase and adapt a car. "By the mid-seventies, grants were available from IWA and the Health Board," says Micheál. "IWA used to give £400 towards the purchase cost and even though the Association was strapped for cash, it would offer loans to members. You just had to come in and see Reggie Scally, who was our money man. All you needed was a hundred pounds and you got a brand new adapted Mini." Members also benefited from support from the Lions Club and from deals with car companies such as Nissan, which allowed them to delay paying a portion of the purchase price until they got VAT and duty back from the Revenue Commissioners. "All these things helped put people on the road," says Micheál, "And fair play to the members, they understood that. If they got a loan, they would be in on a Saturday afternoon to pay Reggie. When members got it in their head that you were trying to do something for them, they would stand by you."

Even with all these supports, purchasing a car remained beyond the reach of many. "Some members were very badly off. You'd never understand unless you'd been into their houses and seen the terrible conditions," says Micheál. Paddy used his fundraising connections to encourage the public to donate cars. "I got to know the horsey crowd," he says, "and we got lots of cars from them, or people would donate a car when a relative died. Someone could always use it, so I used to drive around the country collecting cars and handing them out to members."

Micheál says funding the driving school was an ongoing challenge. "We always had a problem with money but somehow we managed to scrape things together. I remember one day a woman came in asking for me. The girls in the office thought it must be a complaint, but when she sat down she said, 'I've a cheque for you,' and passed me a cheque for £20,000!" The driving school got its biggest financial break in late 1994 when former MEP Richie Ryan approved funding. "We'd explained that we were a national outfit, not a narrow-minded Dublin outfit. And he gave us £132,000 to keep the driving school going. I remember getting on to our members to tell them to stop writing to ministers, TDs and councillors because we were going to be looked after."

"As more and more people were seen driving, it had a knock-on effect. People would say, 'If he can drive, why can't I?' Sometimes we had to devise complicated solutions, but I could count on one hand the people I turned down"

The aim of the driving school was to get people through their driving test and on to the road. "At one stage there was an issue with the testers over the hand controls. One student would be pushing to brake, the other pulling, and the testers didn't know what was going on. So eventually the supervisors took over and we started to work with them. It was a learning process, finding the right way to do it, but they were excellent. The testers began to understand that there was no point telling a disabled driver to have their hands at 'ten to two' and all that. Paddy and I got to know every one of the testers, and the girl in the office in Ballina, and they'd send new lads out to us for training."

Micheál and Paddy often helped members collect or appraise second-hand cars. "All that counted at the end of the day was the member and if you could do anything at all for them, you'd do it, even if that meant working Saturday or Sunday or any day that God sent," says Micheál. On one occasion, Paddy remembers arriving back at Clontarf after a day's driving and finding one of the members, Vera White, waiting for him. "Vera said, 'You're coming to England with me'. I said, 'I am like hell!' But she wouldn't let me go home so we ended up flying over to Birmingham to see some car she wanted to buy. It was this orange adapted Mini which had been made as a demonstration model in some highly secret military base. It turned out to be the place where they were making the armoured cars for Northern Ireland, and there we were, a couple of Irish people, over to investigate!"

Paddy continued volunteering as a bus driver and helped organise several trips abroad in the 1980s. In 1981, he was part of a team of six guards, three nurses and three drivers (all volunteers) who brought twenty-five members on a two-week trip to France and Germany, where they joined tour buses from other disability organisations. "That was the best trip we ever had," says Paddy. "The volunteers had raised money from dances at the National Ballroom and the Tara Club

in D'Olier Street, and we organised it so nearly everything was free. Before we left, the guards rigged the bus out and the truckers fuelled and washed her. The owner of the filling station in Rosslare filled up the tank, and food was laid out for us on the boat.

ABOVE Paddy Saunders was one of the volunteer drivers on a memorable IWA holiday to France and Germany in 1981. In the days before health and safety legislation, the objective was to bring as many members as possible, although this made toilet stops rather awkward

Wherever we went, we got away with murder because we had the International Police Association Crest on the bus!" The IWA group eventually met up with the other groups and toured for a while, staying in campsites. "The only problem," laughs Paddy, "was that we couldn't keep up with the other buses. Our bus was so old and so packed that if someone needed the toilet, we'd have to stop for half an hour because the person could be at the back of the bus and everyone else would have to unload to let them off."

Paddy and Micheál are proud of their work. "I used to keep a list of all the members we taught to drive, the time they passed their test and the type of car they got," says Micheál. "As more and more people were seen driving, it had a knock-on effect. People would say, 'If he can drive, why can't I?' Sometimes we had to devise complicated solutions, but I could count on one hand the people I turned down, and I'd say you're the same, Paddy." Looking back, Paddy and Micheál say the way they did things wouldn't be possible today. "There are too many health and safety regulations. Back then, we followed a simple rule: Never ask anybody to do what you are not prepared to do yourself. We had no degrees or qualifications but the results are on the road, that's the way we see it. We always had great time for all our members, and for the effort they had to put in to do what we took for granted."

Paddy retired from IWA in 1999 and Micheál in 2001. They both live in Dublin.

Jimmy Byrne

Encouraging and inspiring young people through sport and holidays

Jimmy Byrne is regarded by many IWA members as a father figure, someone who has spent a great deal of time encouraging and supporting young members and athletes during his forty years with the Association. While Jimmy is too modest to describe himself in these terms, he says, "The Association has been part of my family's life for over four decades and I have a very personal relationship with lots of people in IWA, particularly the members I've watched grow up over the years. I officially retired in 2004 but I keep coming back. I'm still coaching several athletes and I am company secretary for IWA. I suppose if it were just business, I would have been gone years ago!"

Jimmy became involved in IWA in 1969 through his brother, Paddy, and he says that for several years he was known simply as 'Paddy's brother'. "Paddy was a young garda in Store Street when he started volunteering. At that time it was unusual for a Dubliner to be in the Gardaí, and particularly to be stationed in what was considered a fairly rough area. We lived around the corner from the station, in North Strand, so Paddy would be called on at all hours. Paddy was one of many gardaí recruited by Mrs Dowling to drive members to the socials and help organise holidays. He'd ring me and ask me to assist with various things and that was how it all started for me." At that time, Jimmy was working as a service engineer with an oil company and had moved to Killester with his wife, Una. "Being involved in IWA," says Jimmy, "was like being a member of a club. I never saw it as charity work and neither did Paddy. It was the same as being part of a football or golf club, because we got so much out of it as well. I think Paddy felt that people with disabilities were entitled to more. When you saw the situations people were in, it was impossible not to feel that. The way it was in those days, some people wouldn't get out of the house all month unless someone called to take them out.

"These days, people associate me with sport, but I got involved through the Dublin holidays," says Jimmy. "Paddy roped me in to do bits and pieces on holidays in St Paul's School in Raheny and Chanel College in Coolock. Then, in the early seventies, I was asked to do a full holiday in Newpark School in Blackrock. Newpark had just been built and had a swimming

RIGHT Children enjoying an IWA summer holiday at St Paul's secondary school in Raheny, Dublin, around 1980. Jimmy was one of many volunteers who made such holidays possible

pool. I remember this paraplegic young man from Limerick was on the holiday. He was thirty-three years old but he'd never seen a swimming pool before, and he was like a dog with two tails when he saw it. Nobody had ever thought he would enjoy a pool, never mind want to learn how to swim. I started teaching him and by the end of the holiday he was boasting to everyone that he had learned to swim in a week. I was pretty chuffed to be honest with you. On foot of that I was asked to help out in an IWA swim club in Belvedere College on Monday nights, which was run by Micheál McSharry, the father of one of our members, Miriam McSharry, and I kept going with that for years."

In the mid-1970s, Jimmy volunteered to take a small group of young members on a holiday. "We went over to a Presbyterian college in Wales with other disability groups from the UK. When we got there, we found it all a bit stuffy and the members got annoyed because they felt they were treated like invalids. The local pubs were open very restricted hours, and organisers would always arrange for something to be on at those times. So we decided to lead a mini rebellion, by going out on our bus in the day and making our own entertainment, and before long people from other groups were queuing to come with us. The organisers also got our backs up by telling us that the local Catholic church was at the back of a chip shop and that we probably wouldn't be interested in going there. Normally, church was the last place members wanted to go when on holiday – some of them lived in institutions and had to go to mass everyday – but the organisers' attitude got on our nerves so everyone suddenly decided to make a point and go. When you're away, you get a bit patriotic!"

"I think a lot of the drivers would agree with me that the nicest part of going to Baldoyle was driving out with a bus full of happy kids"

Jimmy helped out with Dublin-based holidays throughout the 1970s and 1980s. "The way the holidays worked was that IWA would take over a school for a couple of weeks in the summer. The classrooms would be turned into dormitories, using beds supplied by the army or Health Board. We'd do our own catering and the senior students would help out. One of the high points for me was seeing teenagers helping with everything from cooking to personal care or writing letters for members. It was wonderful to see youngsters doing all that, especially when you heard the trouble they'd get into at other times. Sometimes parents would drop by and say, 'Is that really my John? He wouldn't wash a cup at home and there he is scrubbing a floor!'

"Another thing that stuck in my mind," says Jimmy, "was that during the holiday it might take two helpers to transfer someone from their wheelchair into bed. And yet when the holiday was finished, I would leave them home and there might be a little old lady, five foot high, who would answer the front door and say, 'Thank you very much. You're very good'. And I'd be driving away thinking, how in the name of God does she manage for the other fifty weeks of the year? It embarrassed me when people said I was good, because it was people like that who were doing the real work."

On one or two Sundays a month, Jimmy was one of many volunteer drivers who collected members and brought them to IWA's 'Southside Social'. "At 12.30pm, I would collect a lady and bring her from Templeogue to Sion Hill Convent in Blackrock, where the social took place. The lady never got out of bed, so she would be pushed out of her room in her bed and up a hinged ramp into our van. My eldest daughter, Deirdre, came with me and would sit in the back and hold on to her bed for the whole journey to stop her rolling around. We would drop her off at the school and then pick up a couple more people in the area. The Southside Socials were organised with great efficiency by a Ladies Committee. Some of the ladies from the committee would come dressed in evening wear. They would distribute badges to members on arrival to confirm they were entitled to tea. The entertainment could be good or bad, but members looked forward to it all week. One day you might have showband legends like Sonny Knowles or Red Hurley and the next it could be a poetry reading. Either way, they had a captive audience!"

Jimmy also became involved in St Mary's Hospital, Baldoyle. "When I first started going to Baldoyle, I felt I was in a strict institutional environment. While some of the children were there for educational purposes, many had never experienced living in a family home. Life was not easy for them. After a while, some of the kids started calling me 'Daddy' and asking Una and me to adopt them. The children saw me as someone to share their problems with and I found it hard not to become attached to individual children. The most poignant thing of all was when you went in and asked where a particular child was and were told, 'Ah, he died last week'. But it wouldn't be fair to say it was always sad; there were happy times too.

"My main involvement in Baldoyle was through sport and as a volunteer driver. I think a lot of the drivers would agree with me that the nicest part of going to Baldoyle was driving out with a bus full of happy kids. As soon as we were on our way, the singing would start. Some of the songs they sang would make a rugby song sound like an altar boys' chorus. Trips could be to sports events, IWA socials, parties or even the St Patrick's Day parade – any reason to get out was seized upon. At Christmas time, I would drive the kids to parties organised by local factories and social clubs, where there would be all sorts of goodies and sweets. My kids used to love it, because I'd go straight home afterwards and they'd sneak into the bus and go scavenging, finding boxes of Smarties and other sweets that the Baldoyle kids had dropped.

"The priority for me was to see the kids integrated into the community, and sport was a great way of doing that. Martin Naughton became the driving force behind sport in Baldoyle, setting up clubs and encouraging links with the local community. He was a very positive influence on the place and a great motivator. I remember one time Baldoyle hosted the junior games and Martin had the whole local community working on the event. He'd even managed to get wine sponsored for the adults!"

Jimmy believes sport helped raise the aspirations of the children in Baldoyle. "In the early years, it used to sadden me when a teenager would ask me to help them get into a particular Cheshire Home. I was sad because that was the height of their expectations or ambition for the future. Sport was one of the things that helped to change this. Quite a few kids who started sport in Baldoyle later went on to represent Ireland at international and paralympic level. Another positive development was the opening of IWA independent living units in the late eighties, because they offered a way of making the transition from institutional to mainstream living."

Jimmy adds that to this day he often comes across people from Baldoyle. "I love meeting people whom I first met as children in Baldoyle. We talk of old times, have a laugh, and sometime a little weep. They tell me what they are doing now, and in some cases introduce me to their children and spouses."

Baldoyle was just one place in which Jimmy says he witnessed the

LEFT Coaches and support staff for the Irish Paralympic Team in 1980. Back Row (l to r): Derrick Weir, Carmel Begley, Roisin McConnell, Carol Hayes, Mick Noonan and Jimmy Byrne. Front Row: Paddy Finn and Dr Barra O Tuama

power of sport as "a vehicle for integration". Gradually, IWA athletes started competing in integrated leagues, like the Leinster Table Tennis League, and at mainstream venues like Santry Stadium. "The Dublin Marathon was another example," says Jimmy. "Athletes with disabilities weren't allowed to compete in the first Dublin Marathon in 1980, but after some negotiation, we were accepted into the second Dublin Marathon in 1981, and Michael Cunningham became the first wheelchair winner. And then Gerry O'Rourke went on to win so many times that he became a household name, so much so that when John Fulham was racing years later, people used to shout, 'Come on, Gerry!' People started to acknowledge wheelchair athletes as serious athletes, and became interested in their successes, rather than just wanting to know how they'd got their disability."

The concept of integration also began to influence IWA's approach to holidays. "By the late eighties, the idea of integrated youth holidays had taken off. Groups of thirty or forty members would go to Mosney, Trabolgan or other adventure centres. In the morning and afternoon we'd have set arrangements, but after that members were free to take part in anything. For many kids, it was their first time away from home in a non-hospital environment, and they really came out of themselves. We depended on a core of volunteers and I'll never forget one young helper on a holiday in Mosney. I asked him to make sure that one of the children got turned three times a night, and he said, 'Yeah, yeah. No problem.' That night when I went round checking on everyone, I couldn't open the door to his chalet because he was asleep on the floor behind it. He told me he hadn't wanted to go to bed in case he didn't wake up to turn the child. Things like that made an impression on me."

In the 1980s, Jimmy says that sport began to be visibly professionalised. "Anne Ebbs was appointed as Director of Sport and the opening of the IWA sports hall in Clontarf was a big plus. Basketball players, for example, could now wheel in, play a game, have a shower, and wheel out. IWA was in a bigger league and could host basketball and table tennis tournaments that would be attended by thirty different countries. With better training facilities and increased competition, athletes started to move away from 'multi-sport' and become more sports-specific, taking their chosen sport to a more serious level. Our national championships reflected this trend as we started devoting a full weekend to each sport and attracting competitors from abroad."

In 1990, after twenty years as a volunteer, Jimmy became IWA's first full-time Sports Co-ordinator, a position he held until his retirement in 2004. During that time, he helped pioneer an integrated coaching programme through the National Coaching and Training Centre in Limerick. "The idea was to ensure that every coaching manual and course, whether it was in the GAA, FAI, IRFU, or whatever, would include a module on coaching a person with a disability. It took years, but most organisations took it on eventually, and now it's mandatory. To me this is great progress. It means that wherever you live, if you push into your local club, the coach won't say, 'What am I going to do now?' He'll have a manual

ABOVE Jimmy meets the Prince of Wales at the opening of the Olympic Village in Stoke Mandeville in 1981. The Olympic Village was built to provide accommodation for athletes at the 1984 Paralympics which were partly held in Stoke Mandeville

and a number he can ring for advice. I don't believe there was ever a deliberate exclusion policy; it was just a fear of the unknown."

Having coached athletes for every Paralympic Games since 1976, Jimmy was selected as Ireland's Chef de Mission at Beijing in 2008. "It was a great honour and meant a lot to me. When I was over there, I started to think about how far we had come since the early days. We used to collect in shopping centres and churches to raise the money to travel. Now athletes are funded year-round and receive travel and equipment expenses. It's a far cry from the days when my wife Una used to go round looking for green shirts in Dunnes Stores, or from when we used to sleep on floors in gyms! Some of the older athletes will tell you that when we were away at events, we used to go into restaurants and I'd say, 'You can have what you like, lads, as long as it's chips and eggs!' Today, it's a different world. For a small country, we have punched above our weight at a paralympic level and now our athletes are getting the recognition they deserve."

ABOVE Jimmy's brother, Paddy, a garda in Store Street, Dublin 1. Paddy became a committed volunteer in the late 1960s, working to support socials, holidays and the setting-up of local branches

Proud as he is of Ireland's paralympic success, Jimmy believes sport is about much more than medals. "My thing is that athletes should reach their full potential. It might take one swimmer two minutes to do a length, and another a third of that time, but as long as they are both working to their full potential, it's an achievement. It gives me a buzz to see people enjoying sport and achieving their goals. It gets people out of themselves, younger people in particular. I'm proud of the number of people I've influenced to become involved in sport. And it's great to see some of them, like Mark Barry and Garreth Greene, working in IWA today, encouraging the next generation to play sport."

"It gives me a buzz to see people enjoying sport and achieving their goals. It gets people out of themselves, younger people in particular. I'm proud of the number of people I've influenced to become involved in sport"

In sport, and in other areas, Jimmy believes that life for people with disabilities has changed dramatically over the forty years in which he has worked with IWA. "The simplest way I'd put it is that people with disabilities won't accept second best anymore, and that is a great credit to themselves and to the organisation. They expect to be able to live independently and access proper support services, to be able to drive, and if they play sport, they expect world class facilities. I've seen it first hand and I know I'd much rather be in a wheelchair now than forty years ago."

Jimmy and Una live in Killester. They had one son (who sadly passed away) and four daughters, and now have eleven grandchildren. Jimmy's brother, Paddy, left the Gardaí to become a full-time IWA employee in the late 1970s. Paddy passed away in 1988.

Protesting outside Leinster House in March 1995

Irish Wheelchair Association in the

1990s

LEFT **Founder member Jack Kerrigan welcomes President Dr Patrick Hillery who officially opened the International Writers' workshop in Mornington** ABOVE **Founding members Oliver Murphy, Kay Hayes and Jack Kerrigan at an IWA Christmas party** BELOW **A team of fundraising walkers in the Holy Land, 1990**

1990   **1991**   **1992**

MARCH 1990
Building Control Act

In March 1990, the Minister for the Environment, Padraig Flynn, TD, announced measures to improve access to new public buildings. The provisions were contained in the Building Control Act of 1990, however the Act was not fully enforced until 1992. Despite this, the announcement of the measures was a major step forward for people with physical disabilities who had been battling Ireland's inaccessible built environment for decades. The Act covered entrances, lifts, toilet facilities and internal layout in all state and local authority buildings, as well as privately owned buildings such as hotels and cinemas.

APRIL 1990
Holy Land Walk

On April 28th, 1990, a group of a hundred walkers left Dublin Airport for Israel, in order to raise funds for the Irish Wheelchair Association. The hundred-mile walk took the group of IWA members, staff and supporters to such places as Tel Aviv, Nazareth, Mount Beatitudes and the River Jordan.

OCTOBER 1990
International Writers' Workshop

The creative writing workshops which were held by IWA in 1987 proved popular amongst members and as a result an International Writers' Workshop was held in Mornington,

County Louth, from October 27th to November 8th, 1990. It was attended by IWA members and by wheelchair users from a number of EU countries, including Holland, Denmark, Portugal and the UK.

NOVEMBER 1990
30th anniversary celebrations

IWA members, volunteers and staff from all over the country gathered in the Mansion House in Dublin to celebrate thirty years of the Irish Wheelchair Association, on November 5th, 1990. Among those who attended that evening was President Mary Robinson who had represented Liam Maguire in his landmark case against the State some years earlier. Guests of honour included three of the founder members, Jack Kerrigan, Kay Hayes and Oliver Murphy.

MAY 1991
President Mary Robinson attends National Sports Championships

The National Sports Championships were traditionally held over the Whit bank holiday weekend. All sports would have competitions running simultaneously: athletics in Morton Stadium in Santry; swimming in St Paul's, Raheny; table tennis in the IWA sports centre

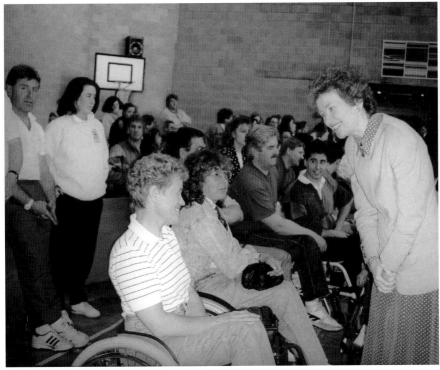

LEFT **President Robinson chats to athletes at the IWA National Sports Championships**
ABOVE **The Cathaoirleach of the Seanad, Sean Fallon, outside Leinster House on February 18th, 1993 to welcome new member, Senator Brian Crowley, with Senator Brian Hillery, Senator Don Lydon and Senator Donie Cassidy (Pic courtesy of *The Irish Times*)**
BELOW **First edition of *Spokeout* Spring 1992**

1993   1994

in Clontarf; and snooker and archery in various locations throughout Dublin. Many international competitors would travel to Dublin for these events. On the final day of the championships, when all competitions were complete and the selectors meetings were finalised, the Chairman of IWA Sports Jimmy Byrne would announce the Irish National Team.

In 1991, President Mary Robinson visited the National Championships on the Sunday morning and was able to watch the final match in both the mens and ladies table tennis.

MARCH 1992
First edition of *Spokeout* magazine

The first edition of *Spokeout* magazine, IWA's membership magazine, was printed in Spring 1992. The introduction to the first issue explained: "The name of the magazine is intended to represent a lot of what the magazine is about and can be interpreted in three ways. Firstly, the most obvious connection is between 'spoke' and the main method of transport for the majority of readers with disabilities, the wheelchair and its spokes. Secondly, it is intended that the magazine will remain a medium through which people with physical disabilities can 'speak out' about issues of importance to them. Finally, for most readers, disability forms part of their lives, but by no means all of it. Spokes going out beyond disability issues represent people with disabilities' wider interest in the community." Spokeout replaced a series of newsletters published by IWA in the 1980s, which had in turn replaced IWA's first magazine *Push*, which had been published in the 1960s and 1970s.

SEPTEMBER 1992
The Barcelona Paralympics

Ireland sent a large team to the 1992 Paralympics in Barcelona. The stadiums and the purpose-built athletes' village, which included its own beach, were praised by the Irish team. The standard of competition had leapt forward and many world records tumbled during these games. Spanish locals flocked to the stadiums each evening and the BBC also started to provide daily coverage of the event. The Irish team's successes included Siobhan Callanan and Esther Stynes winning a silver medal in the ladies table tennis team event.

FEBRUARY 1993
Brian Crowley elected to Senate

Brian Crowley became the first wheelchair user in the Irish Senate in spring 1993. He received a nomination from Taoiseach Albert Reynolds. Speaking in an interview with Spokeout magazine he said, "Access is a huge problem still and my appointment will really bring that to the forefront."

DECEMBER 1993
Start of Interact project

In December 1993, Michael Woods, TD, Minister for Social Welfare, approved IWA's community development project, known as 'Interact'. With initial funding of €200,000, the project aimed to enable people with disabilities to participate in their local communities. This project, which later became known as 'Interaction', would continue until the mid-2000s.

APRIL 1994
People First report on members' needs

By the late 1980s, it had become evident that there was a serious information deficit in terms of data held by the Association on its membership. A survey and database project was initiated to gather information on

LEFT **Members of the Irish wheechair track and road racing squad in the mid-1990s** ABOVE **Athlete Seán O'Grady** BELOW **Protesting outside Leinster House in March 1995**

1995   **1996**   **1997**

members. The outcomes of this survey were published in the report *People First* in April 1994.

Among its findings, People First showed that much work was still needed on the integration of people with disabilities in the community. Findings revealed that 72.5 percent of members were unemployed, and that 50 percent were found to have no involvement in social activities outside the home.

The report also outlined priority areas for members, including advocating for improved benefits and services, developing programmes that would deal with physical barriers to accessibility, influencing public attitudes, ensuring equal access to education and improving social contact.

MARCH 1995
Launch of peer counselling service
Peer counselling had long been available within the Association on an informal and voluntary basis, but in March 1995, the service was professionalised and officially launched by President Mary Robinson.

New counsellors, all of whom had a physical disability, completed training as part of a joint

programme between IWA and the National Council for the Blind (NCBI). The service enabled people with disabilities to discuss issues that were of concern to them with a counsellor who shared first-hand experience of living with a disability. Before the service even began, sixty people had expressed their interest in availing of it, and by 1996, an additional sixteen counsellors had been trained.

MARCH 1995
Protest at lack of funding for services
On March 21st, 1995, IWA organised a march across the city centre to Leinster House. Protestors handed a letter to Taoiseach John Bruton calling for a specific Government commitment to services for people with physical disabilities, and condemning the £2 million allocation in the budget estimates as paltry.

Soon after, the Minister for Health, Michael Noonan, TD, announced that a further £2.5 million in capital funds would be added to the £2 million already promised. This money would be used to develop services such as home and day care, community-based therapy, residential care, and technical aids and appliances.

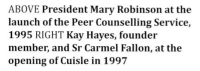

ABOVE **President Mary Robinson at the launch of the Peer Counselling Service, 1995** RIGHT **Kay Hayes, founder member, and Sr Carmel Fallon, at the opening of Cuisle in 1997**

1998

1999

OCTOBER 1995
Personal Assistants programme
The operation of the Personal Assistants (PA) programme was incorporated into the Association in October 1995 at the request of the Department of Health. This programme had been pioneered in Ireland by the Center [sic] for Independent Living.

The PA programme, in conjunction with IWA's existing Home Care Attendant service, would evolve into the Assisted Living Service, which operates throughout Ireland to this day. The service, which provides PAs to assist people with disabilities in carrying out daily tasks, made independent living an option for many people with disabilities who had previously lived in institutions. A fundamental principle of the PA service was that while the Association offered training and support, people with disabilities managed the operation of their PA service.

AUGUST 1996
The Atlanta Paralympics
The 1996 Paralympic Games were held on August 16th - 27th, 1996, in the high temperatures of Atlanta, Georgia. The American organisers put on an amazing opening ceremony that included a good luck speech from Christopher Reeve. Among the Irish winners were IWA athletes David Malone, who took home silver in the 100-metre backstroke, Seán O'Grady, who won bronze in the discus event, and Gráinne Barrett-Condron, who won bronze in shot-putt.

JUNE 1997
Cuisle Holiday Centre
Providing holidays for members had been an integral part of the Association since its foundation, and in 1995 IWA began to explore the possibility of developing a national accessible holiday and respite facility at Donamon Castle in Roscommon. It was hoped that such a facility would meet the increasing demand for respite services amongst IWA's membership.

The project involved an intensive refurbishment of an existing building provided by the Divine Word Missionaries. In June 1997, Cuisle (meaning 'pulse of life') Holiday Centre was officially opened by President Mary Robinson. In its first six months of operation, the centre provided 4,000 bed nights of respite and holidays for 1,600 people with disabilities.

JULY 1998
New IWA training centre
A new training centre was completed in 1998 to accommodate IWA's expanding training department. Prior to this, training programmes had operated out of the day care centre in Clontarf. The IWA training department also gained recognition from the National Accreditation Committee (NAC), confirming that it met the European Union's administrative and training standards. Two programmes operated from the centre. The first was 'TOP' (Training Opportunity Programme), which consisted of modules in advocacy, leisure, arts and culture, remedial education, home management, community placement and basic office skills. The second programme was a Level 1 course covering personal development, job seeking skills, work experience, business and career planning.

NOVEMBER 1999
Opening of administration building, Clontarf
On November 19th, 1999, Mary Wallace, TD, Minister of State, officially opened the administration building in Clontarf. This building replaced the prefabricated building which had been in use since the 1960s.

Patrice Dockery

A positive and committed track athlete

In 2008, Patrice Dockery retired at the age of thirty-seven after a twenty-five year career as a track athlete. Patrice attributes much of her success in sport, and in life in general, to the support of those around her, including other IWA athletes, her friends, her husband and, in particular, her parents. "My parents were very forward thinking and did everything they could to give me the best start in life. If you have good parents behind you and driving you on, I think you are sorted, I really do." Patrice was born with spina bifida and went to school in the Central Remedial Clinic until she was nine. "The CRC empowered me with everything I needed, and it just came to the stage where the staff said to my parents, 'She's equipped now. Let's take her out and put her in a mainstream school – if she needs anything she can come back to us.' So I was taken out and put in our local school. It was a big thing, but I'm very much of the opinion that if children can move into an able-bodied environment, that is the way to go – not only for them but for the other children in the school. My mam and dad were always hoping that my future would involve working, so they wanted an integrated environment to become the norm.

"My parents treated me the same as my sister, Judi, who is three years younger. They threw us both into sports and music, thinking it would be good for us socially. My mam knew Christy O'Neill, who ran a junior sports club, and he encouraged my parents to bring me down to IWA Clontarf when I was about nine. They didn't know whether I would be any good, but they wanted me to get involved in sport because my confidence was fairly low.

"Looking back, when I was growing up, I didn't know a lot about my disability, and ignorance was bliss. My parents made all the hard decisions regarding schooling and medical intervention. My biggest operation was my spinal fusion. When I was around nine, my parents noticed I was getting a curve and brought me to see a surgeon, Mr McManus. I started preparatory treatment straight away, including traction to make my spine more supple, and had the operation at fourteen. Operating was a big risk, and I'll always remember the night before, the surgeon came in and told me not to worry because my mam and dad had made the right decision. And I have to say that I wouldn't have been the athlete I turned out to be without that operation, not to mention the health issues I might have faced later in life."

Around this time, Patrice's mother was diagnosed with breast cancer. "She was going through all that while looking after me. It's not until you are an adult that you realise what was done for you. She was a very strong woman. I had a lovely combination because my dad is an easygoing character, whereas my mam was a very determined woman. I was never mollycoddled by either of my parents, and at times I thought my mam was being hard on me. For example, when she picked me up from school, she'd make me put my own wheelchair in the car. I see now that was her way of preparing me, of making me independent – and independence is the greatest thing you can give a child.

"When they dropped me to IWA in Clontarf, we'd see athletes driving up, getting their chairs out, and wheeling down to start training, with all the social banter going on around them. That's what they wanted for me. I'm sure they were inspired; I certainly was. Athletes like Siobhan Callaghan, Michael Cunningham, John Kelly, Kevin Breen and Gerry O'Rourke became my

ABOVE Patrice with her parents, Maura and Paddy, and her sister, Judith

heroes. The Dublin Marathon used to pass near our house on the Malahide Road and I remember legging it down to see Gerry power past on his way to the finishing line. I get goose pimples just thinking about it! Many of the older athletes nurtured me. Siobhan and Gerry would even drive out to collect me for training sessions when my parents couldn't bring me. It seemed incredible that these paralympians would take time out to spend with a junior. Another athlete who inspired me was Kay McShane from Cork. Kay was a track athlete, and when my mam brought me to Santry Stadium to train, I'd watch Kay going round the track. I remember my mam used to sit in a deck chair at the side of the track, knitting. She'd point to Kay and say, 'Look, that's what you have to do', so I started copying everything Kay did. Before then, I'd always refused to wear a hat in winter, but when Kay explained to me that I had to keep warm, I started wearing one. When Kay said something, I listened."

Patrice's first major competition was the Junior World Championships in Nottingham, England, in 1986. "I won three gold medals and I thought, this is it, this is what I want to do. I loved competing and the lifestyle it offered – the travelling, working to beat my own times and constantly striving to be the best athlete I could be. I was lucky, because around that time I met Mairéad Farquharson, who became my best friend and eventually my coach. We met at secondary school and got on brilliantly from the beginning. I brought her down to IWA and she started volunteering, and then years later, when she'd got all her exams, she became my coach. She also coached many other wheelchair racing athletes including John Fulham [track athlete], and John and I nicknamed her 'MacGyver', after the TV character, because she'd such an eye for bio-mechanics. If she noticed that you were pushing more from the right than from the left, she'd fashion a wedge out of foam and duct tape and shove it in some part of your chair, and next minute you'd be pushing evenly. Mairéad was determined to bring out the best in us. She was my main coach throughout my career and she is one of the main reasons that I achieved the success I did."

Patrice also praises IWA's staff. "I remember when I was sixteen, I came home from my first senior international competition at Stoke Mandeville. I'd done quite well, but I hadn't medalled so I was a bit down. Anne Ebbs, who was Director of Sport, brought me into her office, sat me down and told me that IWA was very proud of what I'd achieved and that I was being too hard on myself. She said there was no way I had reached my full potential at sixteen and she could see a real future for me in elite sport. Those words meant a lot, and that's one example of the way in which IWA looked after my emotional and psychological needs. The other living legend – my 'father' in IWA – is Jimmy Byrne. From a young age, I was very serious about my sport. I remember when I was going off to an international event, I'd meet the other athletes in IWA Clontarf at some ungodly hour, and Jimmy would always be there. As I rolled up the ramp to the bus, he'd say, 'You've trained hard, you've made the team, you'll give it your all', and then he'd give me a wink and say, 'and it's okay if you enjoy yourself!' It didn't matter what result we got in a competition, Jimmy and Anne were always at the airport or ferry port to greet us when we got home.

"My first Paralympics was in 1988 and my last was in 2008," says Patrice. "Over the years, I've had my ups and downs. I came fourth in the 100-metre track in both 1988 and 1996. Barcelona 1992 was difficult because my mam's cancer had come back and she passed away a few months before the Games. By 1999, paralympic sport had become so competitive that we were worried I wouldn't even make the team, so Mairéad and I decided to go to Australia to train intensively for six months. The Australian female track team was the best in the world and I was tired of being a big fish in a small pond. Our strategy worked, as I went from being at the back of the pack to being at the front. I was in peak form for Sydney 2000 and I came sixth in the final of the 5,000 metres while setting a new Irish record, a result I was very happy with. Soon after that, I gave the performance of my career at the European Wheelchair Athletic Championships in June 2001, winning gold at 5,000m, as well as silver in the 800m and bronze in the 100m."

Patrice also had low points. "Athens 2004 was very tough. I fell behind and was lapped, at which point I was involved in a crash. It was devastating – not so much the crash itself as the fact that I had fallen that far behind. I eventually got through it with the support of friends and family, and by saying to myself, 'That wasn't me; I need to get back there and prove myself'. My friends are hugely important to me and without their support, and the support of my husband, Ger, I couldn't have done any of this. Ger and I got married this February but we have been together for nearly ten years and he has always been there for me, training with me on his bike in the Phoenix Park, helping me when I had burnout and believing in me when I didn't believe in myself. And when I was successful, he was so excited, you'd think he'd won the medal!"

At Patrice's final Paralympic Games in Beijing in 2008, she was flag bearer for the Irish team. "What an honour! And even more special because Jimmy Byrne was Chef de Mission. When we were waiting in the tunnel for our moment to come out into the stadium, Jimmy had us so excited; we were singing and reading text messages from people at home. As we came out, I thought my heart was going to pound out of my chest. I felt like I was in the middle of the 5,000 metres, coming into the last 200 metres, when everything matters. I don't think it would have meant as much if I'd had that honour at an earlier point in my career, but I was thirty-seven years old, having attended my first Paralympics at seventeen, and I knew I was going to retire. All my memories were flooding in, and I felt incredibly lucky to be a paralympian.

"After Beijing, I did feel sad about the fact that I had come to the end of my career without medalling at the Paralympics. I went through a phase of thinking I hadn't been a good athlete, but two years later I've come to realise that this was not the case. When you've been an athlete 24/7, retirement can be scary. I had to ask myself the question, 'Who am I now?' My life had revolved around competing, and retiring was like a death; the grieving process was overwhelming. I linked in with a life coach at the Institute of Sport and was put on a programme to help me adjust. I began to understand that while being an athlete was an important part of my life, I was also someone's daughter, sister, wife, friend and colleague.

"Sport is still very much part of me. I remember Jimmy Byrne saying sport is not a privilege of the young, and I love the way IWA has facilities for people at every level. Since I retired, I've started playing tennis and I've returned to basketball. I'm still really competitive, so that's taking care of that end of my psyche! I'm also learning yoga. I started with a class in IWA, and moved on from there to an integrated class in Mountjoy Square. The teacher has gone out of his way to devise equivalents for the positions I can't do, so I'm always part of the flow of the class. Whatever you're into, be it sport, acting or music, it's great to be out there participating in life like everyone else. I rarely experience discrimination and I think that's because previous members of IWA blazed a trail and broke down barriers for the likes of me. Attitudes have improved so much. When people offer me a hand getting into my car, I always say, 'No thanks, I'm grand, but thanks a million for asking'. I don't think people are asking because they feel sorry for me; I think that's simply people looking out for others.

"I've been very lucky throughout my life. I firmly believe that I would have been an international athlete whether or not I'd a disability. It was in my genes. It just happened that wheelchair racing became my sport. The decisions my parents made, and all the amazing people who helped me along the way, just made it easy for me."

Patrice lives in Swords with her husband, Ger O'Rourke [not to be confused with the athlete Gerry O'Rourke]. She is an Executive Officer in the Department of Foreign Affairs. Patrice would like to acknowledge the support of her employers throughout her racing career, her many sponsors, Paralympic Council of Ireland, the Irish Sports Council, the Irish Institute of Sport, the National Coaching and Training Centre and Clonliffe Harriers Athletic Club.

Martin Costello

A disciplined and determined double gold paralympic medallist

In recent years, fifty-two-year-old Martin Costello says he has spent a great deal of time thinking about his childhood in St Mary's Hospital, Baldoyle. "When my mother was alive, I wouldn't have been able to admit how tough it was there because it would have killed her. So I swept a lot of it under the carpet. Then, a few years ago, I was watching a documentary about residential homes for children and I thought, that kind of harsh treatment happened to myself, that happened in Baldoyle." Martin says that after this his feelings about Baldoyle began to impact on his life. "For a while I kept my feelings bottled up inside, but eventually, one of my friends said to me, 'Look it, you're not the Martin I know. You're not out talking to people. You're not up for the craic at hurling matches'. I'd become sort of sombre in myself. He suggested I talk to someone about it all, and since I've started talking, the burden has been lifted."

Martin, who has cerebral palsy, was born in St Mullins, Graiguenamanagh, on the Kilkenny/Carlow border, but says he has always considered himself a Kilkenny man. The fourth youngest of thirteen children, seven boys and six girls, he says his mother was advised to send him to Baldoyle. "She had no choice. I understand that. As well as minding the children, she had to work to keep the house going, cycling twelve miles to Odlums Flour Mill in New Ross every day." During childhood, Martin had to undergo twenty-seven operations. "Most of them were to try to fix my feet, but I also had a couple on my back to straighten up my trunk and give me better balance." Like many other children with disabilities, Martin resented having to wear callipers and splints. "You hadn't a choice. You had to do what you were told." Martin found life at Baldoyle very regimented. "You had to have a shower every morning and wash your feet; then you went for your breakfast and straight off to school. It was a tough place. It was the way children were treated – rough and ready, I'd call it.

"It took me a long time to get used to living 'outside the walls'"

"I was a little devil. I wasn't easy to manage and I accept that. But I got more than I deserved. I remember there was a playroom upstairs called the 'rumpus room'. You'd get locked in there for any misdemeanour. You could be there for an hour and your dinner would be shoved under the door. And if you caused any bother in school, privileges like trips to matches were taken away, and you'd have to watch the other kids pulling faces at you as they went off. To be fair," adds Martin, "there were a couple of nurses who were good to us, and the maintenance men and kitchen staff could be very kind. They'd bring us to matches in Dalymount Park or slip us a few slices of bread."

Martin remembers the day he left Baldoyle in 1974, aged sixteen. "I sat there in the big glass porch waiting for the ambulance to bring me home. I knew I was on my way out, so I was giving the fingers to every nurse who went by. And when the ambulance arrived, I took off my callipers and a horrible old pad that had held them in place, and I said to the ambulance driver, 'These

belong to the matron. Please put them in her office over there!' Martin went home to his mother in Graiguenamanagh. "It took me a long time to get used to living 'outside the walls'. I didn't even know how to use a knife and fork, because I'd always been given spoons to feed myself. I had to be taught everything. My mother used to explain, 'There's a knife. There's a fork. There's a spoon. We do it this way.' She'd be watching me like a child while I ate. My family thought Baldoyle was a palace so I never said anything. I would have hated to upset them. If I'd told my mother, she'd have been devastated, and as far as I'm concerned, she was the best mother in the world. It's just the way life was at that time. I've a fabulous family; all my brothers and sisters worked hard to help my mother when they were old enough, and they've always been very good to me."

In the late 1970s, Martin got a job in a supported workshop in New Ross. "The aim of the workshop was to get people out. I remember they paid us two pounds fifty a week. We'd count little ties for freezer bags. One, two, three," says Martin, remembering the boredom, "and when you got to ten, you'd put them in a little plastic bag. I eventually lost that job after I told the manager what I thought of the place."

"No one can ever take away what I achieved. And the world records stand to this day"

Martin turned to sport as an outlet for his energy. "I'd always loved sport. Micheál Saunders used to bring me from Baldoyle to do recreational sports in the IWA hut in Clontarf. After I moved home, I kept it up on and off, but it was hard because there were no sports facilities down here. Then my mother decided to contact someone in Cerebral Palsy Ireland about setting up a local sports organisation, and that's how I got back into it. I tried all sports but once I was introduced to shot-putt and javelin, I really took to them. I was a strong lad and it appealed to me to see how far I could throw something. 'I'm a man, I can do it!' You do be thinking that way when you're young!"

Martin was selected for the Irish team for the 1988 Paralympics in Seoul and says he had a feeling he would do well. "I knew by the way I was training. I went to bed at 7pm every night and got up early. My trainer was very tough. 'Get out there and do it,' she'd say. 'Don't come back moaning if you don't do well'. She didn't believe in disability. She believed in discipline. 'Nobody remembers if you're second,' she'd say." Martin returned from Seoul with two gold medals – one in shot-putt and one in javelin – as well as two new world records. "I was delighted. I could go home with my head held high," says Martin. "When I got back to Graiguenamanagh, I was brought around the local area in a car, and then we had a big party. To this day, I think of 1988 as my golden year. No one can ever take away what I achieved. And the world records stand to this day. The people of Graiguenamanagh even bought me my first car, because they said I was after putting Graiguenamanagh on the map."

Martin learnt to drive with IWA instructor Micheál Saunders. "I suffered from nerves at the beginning. I used to close my eyes for a few seconds if I thought I was going too near something! 'Will you open your eyes, Martin!' Micheál would say, 'I can't steer the car from my side, I can only stop it!' But I'm driving since and I've never had a crash. My car is my pride and joy and I change it every two years."

By the 1990s, Martin was coming to IWA's Resource Centre in Kilkenny every week. "The staff were very good to me. I got to know Michael Doyle [Regional Director] and Sinéad Foskin. Sinéad was the person who got me on the right road. She told me that IWA was building the Claddagh Court independent living units, and when they opened in 2000 she advised me to give it a go and see how I got on." It took Martin's mother some time to accept the idea of him living independently. "My mother was unhappy about it. 'Do you think he'll be able to manage?' she kept asking. I remember my mum and I were sitting in the old scullery when Sinéad rang to try to convince her I'd be alright. My mum said, 'I'll have to bring his dinner down to him. You know I do everything for him. He's never cooked, and sometimes I have to beat him into the bathroom to wash himself!' That was her way. She was very caring but afraid to let the leash loose. But Sinéad got around her. She said, 'One month. If he's not up to it, he'll be home.' So she had to let me try it.'"

Sinéad advised him: 'Martin, this is it. You are here now. IWA doesn't look after your money; you have to do that. If you spend all your money on horses or go drinking, we won't entertain you. You still have to pay rent. But if you need help budgeting, that's a different story.' That talk was what cracked the whole thing open for me. I needed a bit of straight talking. I was the first resident in Claddagh Court and I'll never forget driving in with all my stuff and Sinéad saying, 'There's your house. There's the keys.' I knew I'd stick it out. I had to."

Martin stayed in Claddagh Court for eight years. "The original intention was that we'd only be there for one year and then the council would house us, but it dragged on. It was unfortunate because we were stopping other people from coming into the units." Eventually, a two-bed house came up in Loughboy. "I moved in two

ABOVE Martin is pictured in his family home in Graiguenamanagh, proudly wearing his two gold medals from the 1988 Paralympic Games in Seoul. Beside him is a collection of his many other sporting awards

years ago and it's a lovely place to live. I'm very house proud. I don't like a dirty sink. I do the housework myself and try to cook healthy meals. I've a sister in Kilkenny and she'll come down and give me a hand sometimes. I've never needed to ask anyone for help, but if I ever fell, it's good to know I could ring IWA and get someone to come out."

Although Martin values his independence, he admits to being lonely at times. "On a Friday, I go home from IWA, I close the door and I don't expect to see anyone until Monday. You do be lonely. I have plenty of friends, and I'd see them if I went into town, but I try to avoid spending too much time drinking in the pub. When you live on your own, you have to get out of the house, so it's very easy to go down to the pub for a couple of pints. I'd love to meet someone and maybe have a serious relationship. I feel that would open up a whole new world for me. Don't get me wrong, I like being independent, but I'm just telling you the other side of it too."

Martin currently works part-time in the reception of IWA Kilkenny and he also volunteers every week. "I do a lot of fundraising, like church gate collections or bag packing in the supermarket. And I count the money for Angel Day – they know they can trust me. IWA has been very good to me so I like to give a bit back. My mum used to say, 'You look after yourself, because nobody else will. Always be fair and mannerly. Admit if you are wrong, apologise and face the music, because you will be trusted and respected for it.' I know I've done very well to get to where I am today, and I also know that without IWA, I wouldn't have got here."

Martin Costello lives in Loughboy, Kilkenny. He loves sports and is a lifelong Liverpool supporter.

Donal Toolan

Actor, broadcaster and disability rights activist

After more than three decades of using a manual wheelchair, Donal Toolan has just taken delivery of his first power chair. "I held off getting a power chair for years, for all sorts of psychological as well as social reasons to do with my perception of a power chair. I went through a similar process to an adult who is coming to terms with using a manual wheelchair for the first time. But now, after a few days of using it, I'm thinking, my goodness, why didn't I do this years ago? It is so liberating. I can do all sorts of things so much more quickly and without expending so much energy."

Donal Toolan was born in 1966, the second youngest of seven children, and grew up in Ballyhaunis, east Mayo. "I have a condition called central core myopathy, although I didn't get that diagnosis until I was a teenager, and it was simply treated as a muscular condition. I was very fortunate to be able to go to my local two-room primary school in east Mayo, although I spent much of my childhood traversing the country between Mayo and the Dublin hospitals." Walking with callipers and braces was so labour-intensive that by the time Donal started secondary school he had decided to start using a manual wheelchair. "When I was twelve and going into secondary school I was very comfortable with the idea of using a wheelchair. I wasn't caught up in all the negative connotations. I just got on with it. It was only in my late teens that I began to be aware of the stigma associated with a wheelchair; the sense of a wheelchair as a signifier of mortality, something that marks you as being physically different, and that our culture says is not normal, not sexy. All these messages happen at a subliminal level and I'm subject to the same kind of conditioning as non-disabled people."

"We still have the hangover of the old way of thinking"

While Donal was unaware of social stigmas as a young child, he says: "When I look retrospectively to my childhood, I realise I had very different experiences from a non-disabled child. It wasn't just all the time spent in hospital, it was the huge discomfort and unspoken discrimination that the adults around me had to face. For example, we lived close to Knock, and I remember visiting one time. I was in my father's arms, and the priest said to my parents, 'I didn't realise you had one like this.' We have photographs of that visit and I was quite young, but I was still old enough to be able to observe my parents' reactions to this comment and the hurt that was visited by it. A lot of that kind of stuff was communicated in a gentle way – that great Irish phrase 'no harm intended' – and I think a lot of it had to do with people's discomfort around disability; the 'candyfloss', caring, not-meaning-to-offend culture that masks the fact that people don't know how to be around those who are different.

"I do think our culture is changing," adds Donal, "although even in the relatively secular era that we're in, we still have the hangover of the old way of thinking, the 'God love them' attitude towards people with disabilities. Interestingly, a lot of the old religiousness did contain a level of empathy, which I think we will also see diminishing. I think we are going to see a new reality for disabled people. You could call it a backlash, but I think what we will see is a competition for empathy amongst many different groups, especially in this economic environment. Disabled people won't enjoy the victim status that was afforded to us in the past, and that will have negatives as well as pluses. It does mean that disabled people are going to have to be more assertive in the years ahead."

Donal sees a number of contradictions in the current culture around disability. "Over the past two or three decades, one of the changes that has affected disabled people's lives is the introduction of rights legislation. Our rights are now set out in law, so that if we encounter discrimination we can use the law to protect ourselves. On one level this has been a huge advance, but what hasn't corresponded with this is the way people receive supports and services, where a charity model still exists. Society is going to have difficulty working out the messages because one day the message is that disabled people should be treated as equal and the next it's that they need charitable support."

Over the past twenty years, the development of Donal's own career has been interwoven with the development of rights legislation. "I came to live in Dublin on the last day of my Leaving Cert, with a vague idea that I wanted to be a journalist or an actor. Within a year or two, I got into Trinity, started a degree in history, was a member of the National Youth Theatre and had started presenting *Not So Different* on RTÉ Radio 1 [the programme which preceded *Outside the Box*]. I was really fortunate in meeting the right people, such as Maureen Gilbert and Bill Meek, but also I had an extraordinary amount of energy, and precociousness perhaps. Not So Different brought me around the country meeting disabled people. One day, disability activist Sean Megahey came on the programme and did a soapbox piece, saying wouldn't it be a good idea if there was a council for the status of people with disabilities. Soon after, I was invited to a gathering at the European Commission, where there were representatives of disability groups from all over Europe. One of the things that struck the Irish delegation was that there was no advocacy group in Ireland that wasn't involved in service delivery, and we thought it would be very useful to do something about it."

In 1990, Donal and a number of other activists came together to establish the Forum of People with Disabilities, an organisation focused on furthering the rights of people with disabilities. The Forum's first campaign focused on the right to vote, tackling the archaic law which obliged postal voters with disabilities to be declared sane by a doctor. The high profile campaign, which included a striking poster designed by artist and activist Mary Duffy asking, 'Are you certified sane?', drew the support of the public and of presidential candidate Mary Robinson. Following the success of that campaign, the Forum began a three-year campaign to establish a Commission on the Status of People with Disabilities. "If disabled people were relatively visible in a media and political sense, you could make a lot of noise," says Donal. "We were saying something new – here's how you should treat people and here's what needs to be in place to make that happen. Within two years of setting up the Forum, we were getting meetings with the Taoiseach to discuss the concept of a Commission on the Status of People with Disabilities, modelled on the Commission on the Status of Women."

The Commission on the Status of People with Disabilities was established in November 1993 by the Minister for Equality and Law Reform, Mervyn Taylor, with the aim of setting out a framework for future legislative policy. The Commission appointed a number of working groups and individuals to develop proposals on issues affecting people with disabilities. Donal says, "Approximately 130 people from all areas and backgrounds were involved in the process, encouraging a view of disability that was very broad. It is important to remember that at that time the general mindset was around a single impairment approach, and what the Commission sought to do was look at disability in a broader context." After three years of consultation, *A Strategy for Equality: Report of the Commission on the Status of People with Disabilities* was published in 1996. "The report covered areas ranging from the built environment to sexuality," says Donal. "It became the template for equality legislation and policy in relation to issues such as housing. Those few years were incredibly dynamic. Disabled people became very visible in the media and were willing to come out and say, 'I've been discriminated against'. It was partly the spirit of the era. Mary Robinson had been elected, homosexuality had been de-criminalised and there was an increased consciousness around Travellers.

"We also benefited from the influence of the EU. You don't get to join a club that evolved in a post-war situation where people's rights, including disabled people's rights, had been so appallingly trampled on, unless you sign up to agreed norms about how we treat people. Many of the legal campaigns that Mary Robinson involved herself in wouldn't have been possible without the EU. When it comes to the EU and the UN, people often say, 'That's way up there, it's nothing to do with us', but actually you will find a direct link with many of our laws and policies.

"Through the efforts of advocacy groups, and our membership of the EU, the situation around how you can uphold your rights has radically changed. Ten years after the report, equal status legislation was in place and the Disability Act was coming into being. That legislation was signalled in the Commission's report, so it has to be seen as part of that path," says Donal. "Today, if I have a situation where my rights are not being met or I'm being discriminated against, the situation is radically different from twenty years ago."

One policy area in which the impact of rights-based legislation is evident is public transport. "The transport infrastructure is now so accessible that I can travel from where I live in Dublin all the way to where I grew up in Mayo. That's a huge change from when I came to live in Dublin twenty-two years ago. We still have a long way to go – the kind of transport we have here now I was using in Germany twenty years ago, so we're only catching up. Historically, the mindset that existed in Ireland in relation to issues like transport was what Roy Keane would describe as the 'Ah, sure, it'll do' mentality. There is a passivity and acceptance in our culture of all sorts of appalling situations."

While great progress has been achieved, Donal is concerned that the disability movement has gone into decline in the last decade – not just in Ireland, but worldwide. "It's inevitable from a cycle point of view. We've had great progress over the past few decades, but we are not yet seeing the next wave of activism. We need to be vigilant because the idea that any law cannot be watered down is naive. We've already seen the equality infrastructure being hugely damaged by the lack of resources. And over the past decade, when we had so many resources at our disposal, we had an opportunity to close down all our institutional settings, and it is an indictment of our country that there are so many disabled people still living in institutions. Another aspect of this is that demographically the largest group of disabled people will be the elderly and we have legally created a situation where there are nursing homes in every village. When I was growing up in Mayo, the notion that people would live in nursing homes was unheard of, and now it's completely normalised. If you consider why older people are living in these situations, it's because the support isn't available at community level. Instead we have supported and incentivised developers to open homes. This is an example of an area in which we have not been vigilant. And this is why in the future I don't necessarily think activism will come from young disabled people alone. I think it will come from middle class older people who expect to live in their communities or with their families, in settings where support can be provided."

RIGHT Donal enjoying taking the mike on an IWA visit to the Garda Rowing Club in Islandbridge

ABOVE Donal in a picture taken to promote his 1993 RTÉ television series *In From the Margins*. This programme received a Jacobs Award and Donal was named 'Broadcast Journalist of the Year'

Donal questions whether residential accommodation is ever the best option. "Nineteen years ago I began to make a documentary where I went to a residential setting to explore whether anyone would live in such a setting by choice. I quickly realised nobody had chosen to live there. Most of them lived there because their house was inaccessible or their family couldn't look after them, or because there was no system of independent living supports available.

"In Sweden, it's practically illegal to have people in an institutional setting. I think there is a level at which we're forgetting the Ryan Report. The whole concept of institutions as we know them is a Victorian one, and in Ireland we were growing institutions long after other countries had accepted they were not a good idea. You often meet people who have been living in residential settings for several decades and there is absolutely no reason why these people couldn't have grown up and now be living in their own communities. It's important to look at how someone arrived at that residential setting. For example, I know a lot of people who went straight from the NRH to a nursing or residential home. If your formative experience of being disabled is being in an institution, then of course it becomes a comfort zone. The outside has been made very difficult to negotiate. What I'm saying is that this shouldn't be your formative experience. If better psychological, emotional and peer supports were available, then I wonder what choices people would make. I don't think I would choose to live in a residential home, but I accept that this is a personal view. I think often the choice is made because it is the best of what's available. If people do choose to live in a residential setting, then they should at least be able to exercise the same basic choices as other citizens, determining when they wish to eat, sleep, bathe or have access to the community, rather than having those activities organised around those who work there.

"There are all sorts of challenges involved in integration but we've known for decades that there is absolutely no reason why people should be segregated," adds Donal. "If the resources we invest in segregation were re-directed, we could achieve a great deal. The cost of keeping someone in a residential setting would pay for an adaptation of a house in a few weeks or months, and the cost of providing PAs is much lower than employing staff in a home.

"It's not easy to move into a community either. The whole concept of independent living has been progressed by the disability movement but I think it is a concept that could benefit from some interrogation – because surely we are all interdependent? You need to be able to get on with those around you, and having support and being able to give support is okay. It's not something I am always comfortable with myself and I have to work at asking for support if and when I need it. Independence is not about a ramp or a few switches on a door, it's about how you interact with your community and how you use community services. Peer support is also very important," says Donal. "I've lots of friends with disabilities and we support each other. There are not enough situations in which people with disabilities come together to support each other. There is a social dimension to this kind of support but also the opportunity to challenge each other in a constructive way and to access the kind of solidarity that comes from a common experience. If you look at the area of sport within IWA, that is one obvious example of the benefit of peer support. People are coming together to compete, but there is also a social dimension, huge camaraderie, and psychological as well as physical benefit. In general, I don't think the whole emotional side of people's experiences has been adequately progressed. For example, it's only relatively recently that psychological supports have become routinely available at the NRH, which is incredible when you think of the trauma experienced. I have observed, by being involved in different activist political groupings, that actually a lot of people who come along to meetings are not interested in the law or in making change happen, but rather in getting support or in sharing their anger. In other words, a lot of people get involved in political activism because there is no other outlet."

Donal says he is concerned at the way in which people with disabilities, and particularly activists with disabilities, can be portrayed in the media. "In 1993, I worked with Maureen Gilbert again on a television series called *In from the Margins*. The programme was based around disabled people telling their own stories, talking about issues such as not being able to get a job, or not being able to get into public buildings. Interestingly, the programme increased participation in advocacy, because at that time people weren't marked as trouble makers for raising these issues. But I think we have gone backwards in some ways. Currently, there is a false positivity in Irish media – everything is about entertaining and there is a fear of being labelled as an activist of any kind. The dominant view of activism is that if you speak up, you are taking a risk."

"There are all sorts of challenges involved in integration but we've known for decades that there is absolutely no reason why people should be segregated"

Looking to the future, Donal says it takes a multiplicity of efforts and approaches to effect change. He sees the convergence of older people's and disability movements as likely. The Forum for People with Disabilities disbanded a couple of years ago "in favour of individual advocacy" and Donal thinks individual legal cases can be very significant. "I'm talking about cases like that taken on behalf of Paul Donoghue in 1996, and that taken by Kathy Sinnott on behalf of her son Jamie in 2001. Although Kathy Sinnott may have lost in law, she won politically, and in terms of media coverage, because people saw the stories and thought, that is unacceptable. The law is not just about the law; it's about making a statement that influences change, not just for you but for others too. Another example is John Doyle's campaign outside Dublin Bus, when he slept out in front of CIÉ, which had just bought a few hundred inaccessible buses. All the media outlets picked up on it. Here was an individual saying, does nobody see what is going on here?"

Donal continues to be involved in activism and the media. A few years ago he worked on the film *Inside I'm Dancing*. "I was consultant in terms of the development of the script and I had a small part in the film. What's interesting actually, if you think of media influencing change, is that the film has been on the Leaving Certificate syllabus for the past two years. And a couple of months ago, on the night of the Leaving Certificate results, I was coming down my road at three o'clock in the morning, after buying a packet of cigarettes, and these two young guys came up behind me, a bit merry, and one of them shouted out to me, 'Hey, you were in Inside I'm Dancing!' I said, 'That's right' (the part I'm in is so small that I don't know how he identified me) and then he said, 'You know I had to take that as one of the films for Leaving Cert media studies. Independent living – way to go!'"

Donal Toolan lives in Dublin and is Chair of International Service Ireland, and is also involved with the European Network for Independent Living.

Dr Oliver Murphy and Shane Barker at the launch of the 50th anniversary stamp at the GPO, Dublin

Irish Wheelchair Association in the

2000s

FAR LEFT **The Chúchulainn statue which was given to IWA volunteers and members during the Millennium Celebrations** LEFT **Gold medallist at the Sydney Paralympic Games, Gabriel Shelley shows his medal to Taoiseach Bertie Ahern, November 2000** ABOVE **Kerry Katona launches the first Angel Campaign in November, 2001, with the help of Erica Murphy from Baldoyle and Nathan Whelan from Swords**

2000   **2001**   **2002**

FEBRUARY 2000
Kilkenny centre opens
IWA's new complex in Kilkenny opened in 2000. The Resource Centre began a daily service to members consisting of co-ordinated training, educational and recreational programmes. The complex also included thirteen independent living apartments and a wheelchair repair workshop.

JUNE 2000
The Equal Status Act 2000
In response to growing activism among people with disabilities, a number of significant changes were brought about in the late 1990s and in the 2000s. The Employment Equality Act, 1998, outlawed discrimination in relation to employment, and the Equal Status Act, 2000, outlawed discrimination in relation to the provision of goods and services. The two Acts were amended by the Equality Act 2004 and eventually became known as the Employment Equality Acts 1998-2008 and the Equal Status Acts, 2000-2008. The Acts prohibit discrimination on nine grounds: gender, marital status, family status, age, disability, race, sexual orientation, religious belief and membership of the Traveller Community.

NOVEMBER 2000
IWA celebrates 40th anniversary
IWA celebrated its 40th Anniversary during 2000 with a special Millennium function in Croke Park on November 4th, 2000. Volunteers and members from all over Ireland came together to represent their counties and were joined by dignitaries from Church and State. Tributes were paid to members, and Chúchulainn awards presented to volunteers. Taoiseach Bertie Ahern commended the spirit of volunteerism in IWA and the magnificent foresight of the founder members.

NOVEMBER 2000
The Sydney Paralympics
The Irish team returned from the Sydney Paralympics on November 1st, 2000. As well as setting several new Irish records and achieving numerous personal bests, team members brought with them an impressive haul of five gold medals, three silver and one bronze. A large press contingent saw hundreds of supporters join friends and family in greeting the thirty-nine-strong team and their coaches at Dublin Airport. Jim McDaid, Minister for Tourism and Sport, welcomed the team home on behalf of the Government.

MARCH 2001
President McAleese visits Clontarf
On March 26th, 2001, President Mary McAleese visited the Association's headquarters where she met staff and members. Ed Jameson, who was in the process of moving into one of the independent living units, had the honour of receiving President McAleese as his first visitor. The President met trainees at the Skillbase training unit and spent an afternoon with members in the Resource Centre.

JULY 2001
Official opening of National Mobility Centre
In July 2001, IWA's Motoring Advice, Assessment and Tuition Service (MAATS) – the new name for IWA's driving school – moved to a new complex known as the National Mobility Centre in Clane, County Kildare. The centre, which co-ordinates services for drivers and passengers with disabilities throughout Ireland, was officially opened by Taoiseach Bertie Ahern, and operates to this day. A number of important functions are carried out from the centre, including the issuing of the Disabled Persons' Parking Permit on behalf of the Department of Transport. In 2001, the centre issued 3,663 parking permits and provided 11,000 hours of driving tuition.

RIGHT **Niall McDonnell in an IWA driving school car at the National Mobility Centre, Clane** ABOVE **Anne Winslow introduces President McAleese to member Florence Dougall** BELOW **Paralympic swimmer David Malone with his silver medal at the Athens Games**

2003 **2004**

The significance of motoring in providing IWA members with increased independence and mobility was as great in the 2000s as it was in the 1960s.

NOVEMBER 2001
First Angel Day campaign
Several new fundraising events were added to the Association's calendar in 2001, including a national fundraising day, 'Angel Day', on November 12th. Based around five specially commissioned angel pins, this event was an instant success, thanks to the help of volunteers, staff, corporate sponsors and celebrities such as Kerry Katona. The first Angel Day raised €190,500 to support essential services. Angel Day is now widely recognised by the public as IWA's main annual fundraiser.

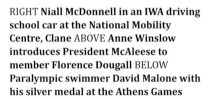

DECEMBER 2003
Clontarf sports and respite centres open
President McAleese officially opened IWA's refurbished and extended sports facilities in Clontarf in December 2003. The Oliver Murphy Sports Centre, named after founder member and sportsman Oliver Murphy, included a workout room with accessible gym equipment,

accessible changing facilities, treatment rooms, office space and a social area. Over two hundred people attended the opening of the centre, including past and present paralympians and sportspeople. In addition to providing sports facilities to athletes with disabilities, IWA's sports facilities were by this stage a valuable resource to local sports clubs, schools and community groups. During the same visit, President McAleese also opened the Carmel Fallon Respite Centre. The centre, which was designed as a home away from home for people with disabilities, offered care assistance and nursing programmes in a friendly environment.

SEPTEMBER 2004
The Athens Paralympics
The 2004 Paralympic Games saw 383 athletes compete from 136 nations. Team Ireland had forty-one representatives, bringing home three silvers and one bronze medal. One of the medal winners was IWA athlete David Malone, who claimed silver in the S8 100m backstroke.

SEPTEMBER 2004
Publication of the Disability Bill
On September 21st, 2004, the Government published the long-awaited Disability Bill, after a twelve-month delay. There was universal agreement amongst the disability sector that significant improvements would have to be made to the Bill if it was to meet the real needs of people with disabilities. IWA, along with other representative organisations, Disability Federation of Ireland and the Not-For-Profit Business Association, presented a formal submission proposing the amendment of the Bill. Despite the many flaws, the Bill delivered on one key recommendation made by the disability sector, namely, that every person with a disability in Ireland would be entitled to a 'statement of need' which outlined exactly what services they required. The key issue with

LEFT **Member Gerard Larkin prepares to get
onto the LUAS** ABOVE **Willie O'Dea, Minister for
Defence, opens Phoenix Lodge in Limerick**
BELOW **Julie Rooney, Clontarf Resource Centre,
tries on the Rose of Tralee's Crown**

2005   2006   2007

the Bill remained the degree to which any
individual had the right to have those needs
met. IWA embarked upon a national campaign
for the modification of the Bill. Lobbying by staff
and members culminated in 2005 with a march
to Government Buildings timed to coincide with
the Dáil vote on the Bill.

JULY 2005
Disability Act (2005)

The Disability Act (2005), which incorporated
suggested amendments by IWA and others from
the disability sector, became law on July 8th,
2005. The Act imposed significant obligations
on Government departments and public bodies
to work towards the improvement of quality of
life for people with disabilities. The Disability
Act advanced and underpinned the
participation of people with disabilities in
society by supporting the provision of
disability-specific services and improving
access to mainstream public services. It
required public bodies to make buildings and
services accessible. It also provided for sectoral
plans in key service areas, and following the
Disability Act, IWA worked to influence the
development of the sectoral plans for each
Government department.

JULY 2006
IWA hosts World Junior Athletics Championships

Athletes from all over the world came to the
Morton Stadium in Santry, Dublin, for the
International Wheelchair and Amputee Sports
Federation's Junior Athletics Championships in
July 2006. One hundred and twenty-seven
junior athletes from seventeen nations
supported by fifty-six coaches and over one
hundred volunteers competed in the event. The
Irish team was well represented with eighteen
Irish athletes aged from twelve to twenty-three
competing in track, discus, shot-putt, javelin
and long jump. This competition was the first
world championships to be held in Ireland.

JUNE 2007
Cuisle celebrates ten successful years

Over five hundred staff and members including
many regular Cuisle guests came together in
June 2007 to celebrate the tenth Anniversary of
IWA's national holiday centre. Celebrations
included a thanksgiving mass, a barbeque and
a charity ball which raised over €60,000 for
Cuisle's Sport and Leisure Fund. Cuisle Holiday
Centre, which is fully accessible, is open year
round and is a welcome destination for many
people with disabilities over the Christmas
period.

NOVEMBER 2007
Opening of Limerick City Housing Project

Independent living apartments, built as part of
the Limerick City Housing Project, were officially

ABOVE **Brendan Close and Bernie Grant at the official opening of the Fr Leo Close Apartments, named after their brother and IWA founder member** RIGHT **Members from Mount Street prepare for the St Patrick's Day parade** BELOW **Jimmy Byrne and Patrice Dockery at the Paralympic Games in Beijing**

2008   **2009**

opened by Minister for Defence Willie O'Dea, TD, in November 2007. The apartments, named Phoenix Lodge by residents, are located in the Sarsfield Park area of Limerick and accommodate six people with physical disabilities.

SEPTEMBER 2008
Paralympic Games Beijing
The Irish team returned from Beijing with five medals: three gold, one silver and one bronze. In addition to this, twenty-five Irish athletes gave performances that represented their personal bests. IWA medalists included Darragh McDonald from Wexford and Gabriel Shelley from Carlow. Jimmy Byrne, who had been involved in IWA Sport since the 1970s, was Chef de Mission and veteran track athlete Patrice Dockery was flag bearer. Comprehensive coverage and results were highlighted in the media and the Irish team also appeared on *The Late Late Show* upon their return to Ireland.

MAY 2009
Launch of the Access Guidelines
Following a consultation process for IWA's Strategic Plan 2008 - 2011 *Your Life Your Way,* it was found that access was the single biggest issue for IWA's members. It was also widely

acknowledged that access issues had a direct impact on other priorities such as employment, housing, parking and transport. In the strategic plan, a commitment was made to develop and publicise IWA Access Guidelines, which would be based upon national and international best practice and cover all aspects of the built environment. The publication of the *Best Practice Access Guidelines* was a fulfilment of that commitment and the publication was launched at the AGM in May 2009.

NOVEMBER 2009
Opening of Fr Leo Close Apartments
An extensive refurbishment project on the Fr Leo Close Apartments in Clontarf was completed in winter 2009. Named after Fr Leo Close, the independent living apartments were officially re-opened on November 10th, 2009, by John Moloney, TD, Minister for Equality, Disability and Mental Health. Funding from Pobal and a generous private benefactor enabled IWA to upgrade the apartments to a high standard.

NOVEMBER 2010
50th anniversary of IWA
IWA celebrated the 50th anniversary of the

Association with a number of events and commemorative activities. Founder member Oliver Murphy featured on a commemorative stamp with young IWA member Shane Barker. He also received an honorary doctorate from the University of Limerick. President Mary McAleese joined Oliver and the founder members' families, IWA members, volunteers and the Board in a special ceremony on November 10th, 2010, held in the Pillar Room of the Mater Hospital.

Terry O'Brien

Family man, Councillor and former Mayor of Tralee

Terry O'Brien is a Kerry County Councillor, a Tralee Town Councillor and three times former Mayor of Tralee. "I am one of a number of people with disabilities in politics, together with people like Brian Crowley and Sean Connick. I like to think if you are after acquiring a disability and you are lying there in hospital watching television, and you see a politician with a disability, you might realise that it's not the end of the world – you can still have a future and a say in society. It's a change of pace and direction, but with the same opportunities to make a difference."

Terry's family have lived in Tralee for generations. "I grew up in Tralee town, but these days I live outside the town, about a mile from where my great grandfather was from." Terry was the youngest of ten children. "I've a twin sister, but she was born just before me, so I'm the baby in the family. When I was growing up, I enjoyed school – the social element and playing on the football team – but at times I would get in trouble for being a bit of a rogue.

"In 1989, when I was twenty, I went to Upstate New York to work on a summer camp as a sports counsellor. It was my second year doing the camp and I had a great summer. I was due to fly back on the August 24th, which was a Thursday, and on the Tuesday before, I dived into a pool and broke my neck. The pool was 4ft deep and I was 6ft 3. You do the maths!" Terry sustained a C5/C6 spinal injury. "As a legal resident in the US, I had health insurance, so at least I got the best of treatment. I stayed in acute care in a New York hospital until the end of October, when I was transferred to the Burke Rehabilitation Centre in White Plains, Upstate New York. I suppose my baptism in disability was in America, where the facilities were much better than in Ireland. I became friends with this guy called Brad, who'd had his accident at a similar time, and I remember one sunny day in March we went out of the hospital in our power chairs. A bus pulled up beside us and a ramp opened out the side of the bus. 'Are you guys coming or what?' the driver called. 'Oh no, sorry, we didn't realise it was a bus stop.' So the ramps folded back in and the bus went on its way. That was in 1990, and when I came back to Ireland the difference was incredible. A ramp on a bus? Are you joking me? More like a plank of wood hanging out the back of a van and a fellow saying, 'Sure, roll up that fast and ye'll be in!'"

In April 1990, Terry returned to Ireland. "I flew back to Dublin on April 13th, Good Friday. As I came through the arrivals hall, I could see all my family waiting for me, but they couldn't see me. It was an emotional moment and lots of spit was swallowed trying to keep the tears down. It was an unusual reaction for me as I was never an emotional kid, but looking back, I understand that it was the first time it became real. I was coming home a different Terry to the one who left. But once I actually met my family, I could see the determination in their eyes to toughen up and take it on the chin."

Armed with this support, Terry went to the National Rehabilitation Hospital in Dun Laoghaire, Dublin, to continue his rehabilitation. "The rehab in America had been good, but in many ways the NRH was better. You could very easily be mollycoddled in the US, whereas in the NRH, although the facilities were not as good, it was, 'Up, up, up. It's time for physio!' The NRH is great but it does feel a bit like a conveyor belt. You go in the front door and come out the back six months later as a fully functioning quadraplegic. I understand that they have to make room for the next person because there is only one rehab hospital in Ireland, but you can't do everything in six months. When I was there, it wasn't that I didn't have any interest in employment or in sexual matters and stuff like that; I just wanted my head right first, without worrying about all that. It's hard to cope when you are a twenty-one-year-old man and everything has changed. You know how when you are a child, you draw a picture of a two-storey house, a man and woman, and two children. No one ever draws a wheelchair. But when you have this type of accident your future is changed completely. Everything you grew up to think of as normality is turned on its head and in six months in hospital, along with getting used to pressure sores, posture problems and using the right type of wheelchair, you have to come to terms with the fact that life is never going to be the same.

"When I came home from the NRH to my parents' house, I was wheeled through the house and out the back door. The dog's shed had gone and they had built a one-bedroom apartment for me. I lived there for ten years, and it worked well because while my parents were nearby, I also had my independence. I was particularly lucky with the friends I had, because they accepted my disability very quickly. I always had one of the lads round at the apartment, watching soccer or messing around. I was never shy about asking for help. I remember in the early days in New York, we had one of those American-style group sessions and the doctor said, 'You will be afterwards as you were before' – in other words, your personality won't change just because you have a disability. I think that's true. I'd always been an outgoing, open person so it made it easier for me to accept help. If I wanted to go to bed, I wouldn't wait for a PA, I'd say to one of the lads, 'Throw me in!' That's the way I've always been."

"I'm not one for roaring or chaining myself to railings. I believe in talking to people and educating them"

In 1991, Terry started a FÁS computer course "as a stepping stone back into some kind of normality". He then went on to study computer science in college. "I wasn't that into computers, but at least I met my wife, Teresa, while I was there. We were friends before we started going out which was very important, and I feel it was good that Teresa didn't know me before my accident, because it made it easier for her to accept me for who I was. Teresa and I got married in 2001 in Bantry. I'm sure some people thought, 'Does she know what she's getting into?' but I think after nine years, she knew. I fell in love with Teresa and she fell in love with me. When I asked her to marry me, we'd already discussed at length all the difficulties. Teresa has her own life, and from day one, I insisted that I had my own care. And I can't criticise the care I receive, I really can't. The support services in Kerry have been top-notch. I have care to help me in the morning, and a PA to assist me at work. Teresa is my wife, that's the important thing to me. At home, I want someone around me who I love and who I'm comfortable with." In 2007, Terry and Teresa had twins, Mark and Millie. "It took us a while to get there and we feel very lucky to have them in our life. We've been very open in saying that we had to have IVF. And it's great to have a contact person in the NRH who will talk you through these issues and make suggestions.

"I always pray that no one in the family will get sick. I remember my mother really wanted me to go to Lourdes when I was in my twenties. On the last night of my visit, I said to my nurse, 'I suppose I'd better say a few prayers. Would you bring me to the Grotto?' I sat there in the Grotto thinking, if there's a miracle going, I wouldn't mind one. Then I saw this child with no arms and no legs, happily smiling away in the arms of her carer, and I thought, look at you, you selfish man. If the Lord had appeared and said, 'You can walk now,' I think I would have wheeled around the back of the Grotto in embarrassment. I was talking to a priest friend of mine afterwards and he said, 'What you got there was peace of mind. You said, 'Yes, I've been dealt a bad hand but I've had twenty years of gallivanting and I've still got a lot of life ahead.' In 2009, I was very sick with septicaemia and it was a tough time for all concerned. I began to question how much more can one take. Sometimes it makes you question whether there is a God, but you have to get on with it. If you start blaming everyone, you'll be there a long time there."

For the past twelve years, Terry has been working as a service coordinator for IWA in Kerry. "When I started, there was only one Resource Centre in Killarney, operating two days a week. All these young people with spinal injuries were going up to Dublin for rehab and coming home to nothing. IWA began to focus on developing more Resource and Outreach Centres, because at least they provide a starting point, somewhere you can go to have a chat or do a course. We also started developing the Assisted Living Services, and disabled people can now do what they want to a large extent. It's made a big difference to people living in rural areas because they can use PAs to improve their quality of life by doing things like going to the cinema or going shopping."

Terry believes one of the biggest issues facing people with disabilities in rural areas is the lack of public transport. "Trains are accessible to a point, and I only know of one operator in Kerry who has an accessible coach/bus. The Government needs to give some incentives to encourage more accessible taxis with proper hydraulic lifts. Maybe they could offer taxi providers the VRT/VAT back, as they do for disabled drivers, but of course it would have to be tightly monitored."

Over the past eleven years, Terry has become involved in local politics. "Dick Spring was a neighbour of mine, and soon after I'd returned home from rehab, he came to visit me, sat down and said, 'What can we do for each other?' Dick and his late sister, Maeve, encouraged me to run as a Labour Town Councillor in 1999 and I got in. Then in 2004, I was elected to both Town and County Councils, a success I repeated in 2009. I've been Mayor of Tralee three times and this is something I am particularly proud of. I get a great buzz out of politics, but you're never off duty. You can't even go for a pint in peace! When I first got elected, the Council Chamber wasn't accessible, but I'm not one to go running to the press with issues like that. I prefer to approach people discreetly and suggest where they might make the necessary changes, and I think people appreciate that. Ireland is an old country with old infrastructure, and while I think public buildings should be accessible, I don't expect miracles overnight. Sometimes I feel the only publicity disabled people get is negative publicity. You hear about someone with a disability who couldn't get off the train, or couldn't get into a pub, but believe me there are positive sides too.

"I'm a big GAA fan and I love to go to Croke Park – and obviously being a Kerry man I am particularly spoilt with the frequency of our visits – but the stadium has a lot of access issues. Groups like IWA and others are quietly working away with Croke Park to improve things, saying, can we develop this or look at that, because I believe that's the way to do business. Of course there are exceptions to that rule, but I'm not one for roaring or chaining myself to railings. I believe in talking to people; it's the way to do business."

Terry emphasises that he is not in politics exclusively to further disability issues. "Obviously I care about disability issues but I don't want to be defined as a disability representative because I've got opinions on plenty of other issues. Sometimes when an access issue comes up, I try to resist getting involved straightaway. We should know about disability, whether we are disabled or not, so while I may interject now and again, I like to let other people talk and learn."

ABOVE Terry and Teresa with their twins, Mark and Millie

Yvonne Fahy

Valuing independence and a home of her own

Yvonne Fahy has a calm and philosophical way of talking about monumental, life-changing events. In her thirty-five years, she has had to come to terms with her parents' separation and her mother's early death, as well as adjust to life with a spinal injury. As she talks, what initially seems like a story of tragedy unfolds into the story of a close and supportive family, and a determination to live independently. Yvonne was born in London, but when she was eight her family returned to the town of Turloughmore, twelve miles outside Galway City. A few years later, her parents separated and she and her brother, Vivian, went to live with their father, while her younger sister, Michelle, stayed with her mother. Yvonne describes herself as the typical 1980s child, obsessed with all things American. "There was no money here; we had a hard old time. We'd uncles and aunts in the US and when we watched the Colbys and the Ewings on TV, with their wealth and lifestyles, we thought everybody lived like that. Like many others, I thought, that will be me one day."

Yvonne's chance came when she was twenty. She moved to Boston and found work as a nanny and then in an Irish bakery. But her carefree life in the US was soon interrupted by news that her mother had been diagnosed with skin cancer. Two weeks later, at the age of forty-one, her mother died. "It was such a shock," recalls Yvonne. "Michelle, who was just thirteen, had to move in with Dad and his new wife, Ann, who was expecting a baby. There was so much to deal with in Ireland and I was all set up in the US. America was my dream, my escape, so I decided to stay there." Although far from home, ties remained strong. Yvonne's sister, Sarah, was born three months prematurely. Yvonne rang home every few days for news.

"I was twenty-five years old and a very private person; the idea of someone you've never met assisting you with personal things is very hard"

"Around the same time, the old Celtic Tiger started to roar and Dad would say, 'Look it, come home'. He'd the option of buying a little shop in Glenamaddy and needed someone to run it. I started to feel lonely. I'd never seen my new little sister, who was pulling through at last, and I suppose I'd never really grieved for my mother." So Yvonne came home and took over the shop in Glenamaddy. "I felt like a fish out of water. I'd left the bright lights of Boston for a country village. I quickly thought, what the hell have I done? The job was stressful and I wasn't mature enough but I couldn't let Dad down and somehow I kept it going. Eventually, I started to settle."

Then, on January 6th, 2000, aged twenty-four, Yvonne had a car accident. She remembers being driven up to Dublin in an ambulance. "The weather was too bad for the helicopter to fly and I remember that never-ending journey. I had a dislocated neck which was held in traction by a 21lbs weight. I remember they let the air out of the tyres to stop the ambulance bouncing. I was in and out of consciousness the whole way." In Dublin's Mater Hospital, Yvonne remembers everything

ABOVE Yvonne and her family at her brother, Vivian's wedding, in October, 2010. Pictured (l to r) are: Sarah, Ann, Vivian, Aideen, John (Yvonne's dad), Michelle, Yvonne and her younger brother, Jonathan

seemed out of control. "There were so many tests and scans and I just kept asking, 'Will I walk?' My Dad, God bless him, brought in a faith healer and it seemed we were making some progress when my right arm started to move. We were looking for any hope at all. After three weeks, it was clear that I would need a wheelchair. I was moved to the NRH in Dun Laoghaire, which had been painted as the next best thing to Lourdes. But I felt so claustrophobic. I'd lie there, watching TV through a mirror, and I felt so trapped that I wanted to scream." Through all this, Yvonne says her family was always there. "It was a good distance from Galway on the buses and must have been very hard for them with work and all, but I was never alone. Even if I wasn't in good form, there'd be someone there, or Dad would have the mobile phone to my ear. I'm far from holy, but I feel like God was on my side."

Yvonne's recovery was slow, with various setbacks, and it was July before she got to go home for the first time. "It started to sink in just how much help I needed. Your family are busy and you don't want to keep asking them to do things for you." After this, Yvonne started going home every second weekend. She found her sister, Michelle, naturally became her carer. "She knew what to do for me without being asked. In one way, it was horrible to think that I was her big sister and now she was acting like mine, but in another way it was great because she made it so much easier for me. I never felt embarrassed about anything."

That Christmas, Yvonne came home for the longest period yet, a couple of weeks, and was given the support of a professional personal assistant (PA). "I didn't know what to make of the whole PA thing – I didn't even know what a PA was! I was twenty-five years old and a very private person; the idea of someone you've never met assisting you with personal things is very hard. But then this fantastic girl arrived and somehow she made it easy for us all." The following spring, Yvonne came home for good. She remembers this as a very frightening experience. "I think I'd become very institutionalised. I was afraid of not having enough money or enough help." But it all came together very quickly. "Everyone – the NRH, my social worker and IWA – seemed to work together very well and within five weeks I was living in an IWA independent living unit with PA support and environmental controls to help me manage the house. Nonetheless, it was hard to have all these people organising my life. I remember a case conference being held before I left the NRH, with everybody talking about my bed, my mattress, my medication. I felt numb, like I was having an out-of-body experience. I'm not giving out – I really appreciate all they did – but it was hard to come to terms with it after being so independent all my life." Over the years, Yvonne has found ways of accepting support while maintaining her own space and privacy. "I now have 24-hour PA assistance but I manage my PAs myself, and I sometimes organise the rota to give me an hour or two on my own and then double up when I need extra support. This gives me space to veg out, blare the radio or have a good sing!"

Yvonne remains close to her sister, Michelle. "I may be physically changed but at the end of the day, it's the same as it always was. I get on her nerves, she ignores me… the same old rubbish. I'm still her big sister. I remember the day she was born; I loved her to bits from the very beginning. She had this cow's lick that we'd spend hours trying to uncurl. She was always destroying my bedroom. She loves to hear those stories." Last summer, Michelle moved to London to work as a make-up artist. "I would never want to hold her back. I get weekly updates on Skype. I don't feel in debt to her but I know I'm awful lucky to have her, and she knows that. I don't want to 'disable' the family, I would feel terrible. I want my little sister to have a fulfilled life. I know she loves it over there, and my plan now is to go and visit her. I also have great admiration for my father," adds Yvonne, "though he drives me cracked sometimes, and I drive him cracked too! But he's always been there for me, through thick and thin. It's the same with my older brother, Vivian, and his wife, Aideen. And, of course my younger sister Sarah, my younger brother Jonathan, and my beautiful little niece Isabelle, are very much part of my life. I love my family but I accept they have their own lives. Maybe I'd feel differently if I had to depend on them for care. I might be angry and bitter." Yvonne believes that having the right external support in terms of housing and assistance has enabled her to maintain balanced family relationships. "I've been very fortunate – the system actually worked for me. It's terrible to think that in this day and age, some people are forced to depend on their families for care. There are enough pressures on families without having to deal with that."

"We always have a good laugh, and that's what it's all about"

In recent years, Yvonne has trained as a peer counsellor and mentor, and has worked in the Citizens Information Centre in Galway. "I didn't feel at all disabled in there. The staff welcomed me with open arms and most of the work was done over the phone so the people I was talking to didn't even know I had a disability. I felt like I had rewound to the time before I became disabled. It gave my confidence a great boost." In June 2009, Yvonne had to give up this job for health reasons. "I hated giving it up. It had taken me a while to get to that stage, and it was very hard to let go. I'd love to go back eventually. Even after a year, the staff keep linking in with me – it's good to know that you haven't been forgotten. At the moment, I'm focusing on getting myself well and keeping positive."

The prospect of Government cuts is one of Yvonne's greatest concerns. "Many people with disabilities live in fear of cutbacks in services and social welfare. Many of us don't have the opportunity to work. My biggest worry is that they could cut my PA hours. I couldn't manage with fewer hours, so that would place me in an impossible situation. The way I see it, I'm saving the Government a fortune by living independently. Having PAs enables me to me get on with life, without affecting anyone else. If I didn't have this support, I couldn't bear the thought of what would happen. It's so important to have your own home." Yvonne believes it is the support of organisations like IWA that enables many people with disabilities to maintain a positive outlook on life. "There are still people out there who don't know what IWA does. It would be fantastic if they would buy this book and learn. The support of IWA means an awful lot. I've been with them since I became disabled and I've never felt like a number. If the services were delivered by the Health Board they'd be putting you on to different people, and you'd have to re-hash your story each time. In IWA, I'm dealing with the same people now who were here when I became a member. IWA is personal, and yet very professional as well."

The sense of community in IWA is also important to Yvonne. "In the early years, I got to know Ronnie Conlon, and I've great respect for him. Such an inspiring and intelligent man. I'd consider him one of my idols. He always said to me, if there was anything on my mind, I could give him a shout. The thing with IWA is, I might not see someone like Ronnie for months but when I meet them, it's like I saw them last week. We always have a good laugh, and that's what it's all about, especially these days. Laughter is great medicine."

Yvonne Fahy lives in Galway. She is a qualified peer counsellor and mentor.

Shane and Theresa Barker

Growing up in an integrated environment

"We're so lucky to have sports people like Patrice Dockery and Mark Barry [IWA Sports Development Officer] in IWA. They are fantastic role models for children like Shane, and for us as parents," says Theresa Barker. "When Shane was born with spina bifida, if my husband Nick and I could have met someone like that, it would have been wonderful. At the beginning, the doctors were telling us that he might not have a very good quality of life. Looking at him now, happy and healthy and always in the thick of things, I think how wrong it was to say that.

"When Shane was born in March 2003, it all happened so quickly. He had to undergo two big operations in the first few weeks of his life. I was upside down but Nick was my rock; he kept very positive. We didn't know anybody with spina bifida at the time and it's only gradually, as you go on and meet people through IWA or whatever, that you begin to get your head around it. And when you see how well he is doing, you realise he has an equal quality of life to his brother and sister.

"Early on, it was easy to get caught up with all the possible complications of his condition. I was researching everything, thinking that I was being responsible. But, do you know what, I gradually realised that if something happens, then we'll deal with it. It's more important for us and for Shane to get on with life.

"If I could offer any advice to new parents of children with disabilities, I would say, yes, there will be difficulties ahead, but disability doesn't have to be a bad thing. Of course, I understand that there are different levels of disability, but I think the best thing would be to have a cup of tea with another parent who knows what it's like to be in that position. Or go down to IWA on a Sunday and see the kids playing in the Swifts Sports Club, and while you are there, look around and see all the older athletes coming and going."

The Swifts Sports Club takes place every Sunday in IWA's Clontarf sports hall. The main co-ordinator is Aidan Knight, whose son, Conall, attends the club, but other parents, like Shane's dad, Nick, take turns to run the weekly

RIGHT Members of the Dublin-based Swifts Sports Club with parents and volunteers. Junior IWA members meet every Sunday for a range of activities co-ordinated by coach Aidan Knight

ABOVE Nick and Theresa Barker with Grace, Shane and Adam

sessions. "Shane loves that club and has so many friends there. He's also done two courses in wheelchair handling skills which were organised by the club. They taught him things like how to go down steps in a wheelchair, and since then he's become so much more confident."

Shane also likes to learn from older athletes. "Kathleen Reynolds is often at the table tennis club on a Sunday and she is great for getting the kids involved. She takes part in games and encourages them. Shane looks up to people like Kathleen, Patrice and Mark. I remember one time we went to a sporting event at Santry Stadium and when it was finished, I said to Shane, 'Come on, get in the car, we've got to go home.' 'No, no', he said, 'I want to wait and see how Mark gets in his car.' That was a few years ago but he was already thinking ahead."

Shane is seven years old and has an older brother, Adam, who is nine, and a younger sister, Grace, who is three. "I think having siblings helps balance the family. We try not to focus on Shane or mollycoddle him. Sometimes I say, 'Off you go into the shop to buy this or that', but I'll be hanging behind the door, sticking my head in to check he's alright. The other day he had spellings to do for school and one task was to incorporate the word 'mother' into a sentence. So he wrote, 'My mother is strict.' I thought, 'Oh my God!' I am conscious of pushing him to be independent and to get on in life. I hope I'm doing the right thing. I do it with all my kids, but life is going to be that little bit more difficult for Shane, so I just want him to be at the top of his game. We live on a housing estate with a big green," adds Theresa. "Even if we won the lottery, I don't think we would move, because it's a fantastic place for the children. Shane is out there every day with his brother and sister, playing football on the green. His main job is playing goalkeeper, or else he'll be referee, going around with his whistle!"

"They taught him things like how to go down steps in a wheelchair, and since then he's become so much more confident"

Shane goes to his local Educate Together School. "It is a fantastic school. The whole ethos of the school is that there are no outsiders, whether we're talking about religion, cultural differences or disability. Their motto is, 'All Different – All Equal'. They make sure Shane is involved in everything. For example, I got some old wheelchairs from members of the Swifts Sports Club and I gave them to the school. They have them out in the yard, so the other kids can have a go in them at break time. The benefit is two-fold: the other children get to experience what it's like to be in a wheelchair and Shane doesn't feel like he's the odd one out. The wheelchairs have turned out to be so popular that there's now a rotation system, and the kids have to ask for a tag if they want to use them! It's funny because somebody walked by the school and said to me, 'There are lots of children in there in wheelchairs, aren't there?' And I said, 'No, actually most of them are just trying them out!'"

As well as his wheelchair, Shane uses splints and crutches to walk. "He normally walks into school with his long splints and crutches and then he changes into his short splints and his wheelchair for the morning, and then back into the long splints to walk home. I've been advised that it's good for his mobility, especially while he's growing, and he is happy to do it at the moment. If he ever wants to stop, obviously we'll listen. You go by your instincts and you hope you are doing the right thing."

Theresa says that Shane's disability has had many positive effects on the family. "I remember a time when disability was unfamiliar and you'd nearly be nervous of talking to people with disabilities, whereas Adam and Grace are very aware of other people with disabilities, and perfectly comfortable to go up and chat to them. I even see the effect in the extended family. My sister-in-law decided to do a special needs course, to become a special needs assistant, and one of my nieces is studying disability as part of her college course. I've also noticed Shane's friends can be very considerate to Shane, by holding doors open for him and things like that. It can become natural for children. Shane himself is conscious of other people who might need a hand. The other day we were in DCU, and a man using crutches had dropped some money and was bending down trying to pick it up. Before I'd even noticed, Shane was over there asking if he needed any help. It struck me that Shane was very tuned in to other people's needs.

"Over the years, Shane has had to have quite a lot of surgery. He's takes it all in his stride, but it kills me every time to leave him in theatre. It brings me back to the beginning of his life, the uncertainty of those first few weeks. That said, Shane has been lucky. He's a very healthy child. Recently he joined the Scouts and I had to fill in a form. It asked whether he had any serious illness, and I wrote: No, he doesn't. Does he have additional needs? Yes, he does.

"Most of the time, Shane is going around doing wheelies or racing down the pavement with the flashing wheels he got at Christmas, but there are times when he says, 'You know, Mam, I wish I could walk,' and I say, 'I know, pet, but I love you the way you are and wouldn't swap you for anyone.' Sometimes he says these things at the very times you are least expecting it. But what can I do but give him a big hug and say, 'I'm sad that you are sad, but I'm not sad because you are the way you are.' It's good he can say these things and I hope I'm giving the right answers. Sometimes Adam makes me laugh because he will say to Shane, 'Think of all the things you can do. You're great at swimming and you don't even have to queue up at Disney World!' And of course, Shane was delighted that he was chosen to appear on the IWA 50th anniversary stamp with Oliver Murphy. I'm not sure whether he realises the full significance of it, but he loved it when the stamp collectors asked him for his autograph. When TV3 interviewed him, he said, 'I want to thank Oliver because he set IWA up, and if he hadn't, I wouldn't have my Sunday sports club.'

"It's funny because we were thinking that we'll have to get round to putting in a downstairs bathroom and bedroom before he gets older, but do you know what, we wouldn't be surprised if by the time we get round to it, he's gone off to college or something! He's always off doing his own thing. Looking to the future, I just hope Shane is happy with life. I don't wish for financial success or anything like that; as long as he's happy with whatever life gives him. And going by the way he is now, I think he will have a full life. Nick and I are both very proud of him, in all that he has achieved to date, and all that we know he will achieve."

Shane and his family live in North County Dublin. Shane is an Aston Villa supporter. For more information about the Dublin Swifts Sports Club, contact IWA on 01 818 6400.

Irish Wheelchair Association Chairpersons, Presidents and Chief Executive Officers

Chairpersons of the Irish Wheelchair Association

2007 - Present	Gerry McMahon
2006 - 2007	Molly Buckley
2004 - 2006	PJ Gorey
2001 - 2004	Molly Buckley
1994 - 2001	Micheal McCabe
1990 - 1994	Frank Mulcahy
1988 - 1990	Colm O Doherty
1985 - 1988	Brian Malone
1982 - 1985	Colm O Doherty
1980 - 1982	Brian Malone
1977 - 1980	Liam Maguire
1974 - 1977	Norman Young
1973 - 1974	Brian Malone
1969 - 1973	Fr Paddy Lewis
1965 - 1969	Oliver Murphy
1964 - 1965	Colm Price
1961 - 1964	Fr Leo Close

Presidents of the Irish Wheelchair Association

2004 - Present	Eileen O'Mahony
2001 - 2004	Harry Ellis
1991 - 2001	Sr Carmel Fallon
1971 - 1991	Lord Dunraven

Chief Executive Officers of the Irish Wheelchair Association

2006 - Present	Kathleen Mc Loughlin
2005 - 2006	Molly Buckley
1990 - 2005	Séamus Thompson
1988 - 1990	Management Committee
	Joan Coffey
	Peter Stokes
	Brendan Garvey
	Brian Harris
Sept - Dec 1987	Phil O'Meachair
May - July 1987	Fergus Lynch
1968 - 1987	Phil O'Meachair

IWA Contacts

National Headquarters

Irish Wheelchair Association

Áras Chúchulainn, Blackheath Drive, Clontarf, Dublin 3

T: 01 818 6400 F: 01 833 3873 E: info@iwa.ie www.iwa.ie

National Mobility Centre

Ballinagappa Road, Clane, Co Kildare

T: 045 893 094 F: 045 989 678 E: maats@iwa.ie

National Holiday Centre Cuisle, Donamon, Co Roscommon

T: 090 666 2277 F: 090 666 2646 E: cuisle@iwa.ie

www.cuisle.com

Regional Centres

Ballinagappa Road, Clane, Co Kildare

T: 045 861 346 F: 045 861 144 E: drclane@iwa.ie

Claddagh Court, College Road, Kilkenny

T: 056 776 2775 F: 056 776 1921 E: kilkenny@iwa.ie

Clonbrusk Resource Centre, Coosan Road, Athlone, Co Westmeath

T: 090 647 1118 F: 090 647 1170 E: athlone@iwa.ie

Nore House, 1st Floor, Bessboro Road, Blackrock, Cork

T: 021 435 0282 F: 021 435 0288 E: cork@iwa.ie

Unit 10, Docklands Business Park, Dock Road, Limerick

T: 061 313 691 F: 061 316 562 E: limerick@iwa.ie

3 - 4 Liscarton Villas, Kells Road, Navan, Co Meath

T: 046 907 2539 F: 046 907 2657 E: navan.admin@iwa.ie

7 Davitt Lane, Castlebar, Co Mayo

T: 094 906 0937 F: 094 906 0830 E: castlebar@iwa.ie

Abbeyville Centre, St Anne's, Sligo

T: 071 915 5522 F: 071 915 5598 E: sligo@iwa.ie

Resource Centres and work locations

Ardee	T: 041 685 3046
Arklow	T: 040 291 311
Athlone	T: 090 647 1118
Athy	T: 059 863 8529
Ballmagar	T: 057 93 500 65
Ballycanew	T: 053 982 522
Bandon	T: 023 88 432 83
Belmullet	T: 097 817 27
Carlow	T: 059 914 0983
Carrick-on-Shannon	T: 071 962 0569
Castlebar	T: 094 906 0937
Cavan	T: 049 437 1212
Clane	T: 045 861 346
Clontarf	T: 01 818 6472
Cork	T: 021 435 0282
Drogheda	T: 041 984 6614
Dun Laoghaire	T: 01 235 5410
Ennis	T: 065 684 4150
Galway (Wellpark)	T: 091 771 550
Kenagh	T: 043 332 2992
Kilkenny	T: 056 776 2775
Kilmacthomas	T: 051 295 655
Letterkenny	T: 074 917 7448
Limerick	T: 061 313 691
Lucan	T: 01 630 2414
Manorcunningham	T: 074 915 7393
Merlin Park, Galway	T: 091 771 552
Mount Street, Dublin	T: 01 400 2849
Mullingar	T: 044 934 7511
Navan	T: 046 907 2539
Portlaoise	T: 057 869 4030
Roscommon	T: 0906 662 277
Roscrea	T: 0505 232 29
Sligo	T: 071 915 5522
Tipperary Town	T: 062 52744
Tralee	T: 066 718 0154
Tuam	T: 093 266 59
Wexford	T: 053 912 4578

Part-time work locations: Balbriggan, Ballina, Ballinasloe, Ballymote, Ballyshannon, Carrick, Cashel, Claremorris, Drombanna, Dungarvan, Enniscrone, Gweedore, Killaloe, Killarney, Kinlough, Listowel, Malin, Mallow, Midleton, Rathfredagh, Skibbereen, Spanish Point, Thurles, Waterford City